# And God Spoke with His People

Sermons from the 1980s by
an East German Pastor

# Werner Krusche

Translated by James S. Currie

*And God Spoke with His People*
ISBN: Softcover 978-1-955581-00-4
Copyright © 2021 by James S. Currie
Originally published as *Und Gott redete mit seinem Volk*. Calwer Verlag Stuttgart, 1990.

All rights reserved. No part of this book may be reproduced or transmitted in any form or by any means, electronic or mechanical, including photocopying, recording, or by any information storage and retrieval system, without permission in writing from the publisher.

**Parson's Porch Books** is an imprint of Parson's Porch & Company (PP&C) in Cleveland, Tennessee. PP&C is an innovative organization which raises money by publishing books of noted authors, representing all genres. Its face and voice is **David Russell Tullock** (dtullock@parsonsporch.com).

Parson's Porch & Company turns books into bread & milk by sharing its profits with the poor.

www.parsonsporch.com

*And God Spoke with His People*

# Preface

In this volume are sermons and addresses by Werner Krusche who was the bishop of the Protestant Church in the province of Saxony, the central office of which is in Magdeburg. In retirement Krusche also preached regularly in various churches in East Germany (the GDR) and in West Germany (FRD). The sermons here come from a shepherd who gathers, comforts, admonishes, builds up, looks after, and protects his people, having been commissioned by the one Good Shepherd, Jesus Christ.

Werner Krusche's gift of preaching lies in his ability to set forth the teachings of the church clearly, often using playful disputes. A Protestant "ABC" is offered here for those who know how to read. While preaching from the biblical context and stories, Krusche goes beyond the narrow sermon text into the wider field of word studies and the history of words of comfort and edification in church hymnody. From this, the bishop's sermons reflect a profound pastoral concern for his congregation as well as serious consideration of their political and social circumstances.

One will not find here political sermons in the sense of a "political soapbox", but firm and clear claims on behalf of the welfare of all people. These are not sermons that have the so-called "Wende" as their starting point, but rather they include notable events of the day, confessing that the gospel of Jesus Christ always has a political component. Political sermons can only be Christ's address on behalf of the city, the people, and the state. Thus, these sermons are also to be read as timeless announcements and reminders of the divine claim of the risen One on all people.

These sermons are reproduced in the order of the biblical texts, whose message takes priority over the events of the day because they must be interpreted in light of God's relationship with the world and the church if one rightly understands that relationship as one of good news.

One may also read these sermons in the sequence in which they were preached if one wants to see, in retrospect, how many references, exhortations, insights anticipate events before they actually occurred. That reflects the explosiveness of every address from God, as is evident in any exegesis of the prophetic books, for they understand their own time in relation to the merciful presence of God, so that God's people are aroused and provoked to glorify God.

In his "Letter at Advent 1989" Werner Krusche names the purpose of life of God's people on earth and in the radical nature of the day: "That the moment of the kingdom when peace and joy laugh (laughs!) for us remains unalterably open, that we can see the world in the light of hope of the second Advent and live in anticipation of the future of the God who comes – as its messengers and instruments – that is what I wish for all of us."

I am grateful to Bishop Krusche that he entrusted me with a collection of sermons and addresses so that I could produce this volume.

I also am grateful to Prof. Dr. Manfred Seitz who graciously and supportively submitted this collection of sermons to the Calwer Verlag for publication.

Finally, I thank Mrs. Gertraud Eyselein of Erlangen for her careful proof-reading.

Rudolf Landau
Schillingstadt, August 1990

# Contents

Preface ..................................................................................... 5
Translator's Introduction ........................................................ 10
Genesis 4:1-16 ........................................................................ 14
   September 5, 1982
   13th Sunday after Trinity Sunday at the Cathedral in Zwickau
Genesis 22:1-14 ...................................................................... 22
   September 18, 1988
   16th Sunday after Trinity Sunday at St. Peter's Church,
   Copenhagen, Denmark
Genesis 28:10-19a .................................................................. 29
   September 4, 1983
   14th Sunday after Trinity Sunday in the Cathedral in
   Magdeburg
Exodus 20:2a & 3 ................................................................... 35
   March 27, 1983
   Palm Sunday at the Salvator Church in Prague on the 500th
   anniversary of Martin Luther's Birth
Numbers 11:4-6, 11-17, 24-29 ............................................... 40
   May 22, 1983
   Pentecost at the Cathedral in Magdeburg
Isaiah 43:1 ............................................................................... 47
   April 26, 1987
   First Sunday after Easter at the City Church in Wittenberg
Isaiah 66:13a ........................................................................... 52
   December 31, 1988
   New Year's Eve at the Cathedral at Magdeburg
Jeremiah 23:5-8 ...................................................................... 60
   November 30, 1986
   1st Sunday in Advent at the Protestant Church
   at Saxau in Breisgau
Jeremiah 29:4-14a ................................................................... 67
   February 10, 1985
   5th Sunday after Epiphany at the Kreuz Church in Dresden
Matthew 14:22-33 .................................................................. 76
   Sermon delivered at the Church Conference – Kirchentag – in
   Erfurt, 1983

Matthew 28:20; II Timothy 2:9 ........................................................... 83
   May 31, 1984
      Ascension of Christ in the Gemarker Church in Wuppertal-Barmen; a service in memory of the Theological Declaration of Barmen, 1934

Luke 1:46-55 ............................................................................................ 88
   November 15, 1989
      Bible Study at the Diocese Convent in Wittenberg

Luke 10:17-20 ....................................................................................... 100
   October 19, 1988
      Sermon on at the Mission Bible School in Malche near Freienwalde

Luke 24:13-35 ....................................................................................... 107
   June 8, 1986
      2nd Sunday after Trinity Sunday in Kassel-Kirchditmold – worship service at the regional Kirchentag

John 5:1-18 ............................................................................................ 115
   October 16, 1977
      19th Sunday after Trinity Sunday in the Cathedral at Magdeburg

John 8:12-14 .......................................................................................... 123
   December 26, 1987
      Second Day of Christmas in Schneeberg in the Ore Mountains

John 21:1-14 .......................................................................................... 130
   April 10, 1983
      Sunday after Easter in the Protestant Health Care Facility in Neinstedt near Quedlinburg

Acts 3:1-10 ............................................................................................. 137
   August 29, 1982
      12th Sunday after Trinity Sunday, in St. Jacob's Church in Schönebeck/Elbe

Acts 12:1-17 ........................................................................................... 144
   September 26, 1982
      16th Sunday after Trinity Sunday at the Conference of the Federal Synod of the Covenant of Protestant Churches in the GDR in Halle

Romans 12:1-2 ............................................................................... 151
   May 23, 1984
      Bible study at the Gathering of the North German Church
      Assembly at the Hainstein Haus in Eisenach
II Corinthians 5:14-21 .................................................................. 158
   March 28, 1986
      Good Friday at the Cathedral in Magdeburg
Galatians 5:1-6 ............................................................................ 166
   October 31, 1988
      Reformation Day Celebration in Würzburg
I Thessalonians 4:1-8 ................................................................... 174
   October 19, 1980
      20th Sunday after Trinity Sunday in the Cathedral in
      Magdeburg
Hebrews 4:14-16 ......................................................................... 182
   February 16, 1986
      1st Sunday in Lent in the Cathedral at Magdeburg
Afterword .................................................................................... 188

# Translator's Introduction

In general, sermons are to be preached at a particular time, in a particular place, for a particular congregation. Based on a particular biblical text, sermons are prepared and delivered in a particular context. However, when that context is different from one's own – a different country, a different language, a different political system – it can be instructive to see how the gospel is delivered. And when the preacher is especially gifted, it is not only instructive, but one finds oneself part of the congregation.

Werner Krusche lived most of his adult life in the former German Democratic Republic (East Germany). He was a Lutheran pastor, scholar, and bishop. He was born in 1917 in the Ore Mountain region (Erzgebirge). His father was a pastor. Wounded in World War II, Krusche began his theological studies in 1943 in Leipzig. After a brief post-war British prison camp, he continued his studies in Bethel, Heidelberg, Göttingen, and Basel, Switzerland (all of them located in the West). Married to Muche Stoevesandt in 1950, they had three children: Andreas, Cornelia, and Friedemann. Krusche earned his doctorate in Heidelberg, his dissertation being on the work of the Holy Spirit in John Calvin (published in 1954 by Vandenhoeck & Ruprecht).

From 1954 on Krusche would live and work in East Germany. From 1954-1958 he served as pastor in Dresden. In 1958 he moved to Lückendorf where he served on the faculty of a Lutheran seminary until 1966. After the death of his first wife, he remarried in 1964 to Helga Goldammer. From 1966-1968 he served on the theological faculty of the University of Leipzig. Then from 1968-1983 Krusche was the bishop of the Protestant church in Saxony, living in Magdeburg. He retired in 1983, but as is seen in this collection of sermons, he continued to preach on occasion. He died July 24, 2009.

He is the author of several works, including his doctoral dissertation, the subject of which was "The Work of the Holy Spirit according to Calvin". In addition to a couple of collections of sermons, in 2007 he published his memoirs. Perhaps one day these, too, will be translated into English.

I first learned of Krusche in 1991 when I spent much of the month of May in the former GDR, searching for a dissertation topic. The Berlin wall had come down in November 1989, and I was fascinated with what the life of the church had been like in a country that had been, for the most part, closed off to the West. Having come across this particular collection of sermons, I wrote Krusche if he would permit me to translate them into English. His response came in the form of a letter in which he graciously agreed. Due to a variety of circumstances, I did not begin the translation until 2020, almost thirty years later!

What intrigued me about this project was the context in which Krusche – and others – sought to be faithful as a pastor, as a bishop, as a preacher in a political context in which there was not only tension, but often outright conflict between the church and governmental authorities. It was not unusual, for example, to have East German secret police (the Stasi) sitting in worship, not to worship but to listen for anything that might be construed as undermining or threatening to the government. Nor was it uncommon for there to be informants in the community or even in the congregation who worked on behalf of the government or the StasI. Phones were tapped, suspicious persons would be followed.

By no means was Krusche the only clergyman who remained faithful to his call to discipleship in uncertain, and sometimes dangerous, times. There were many others.

As a retired pastor in the United States, I find it difficult to imagine what it would be like to live and work and preach in that authoritarian environment. As I worked on this translation, I tried to imagine myself both in Krusche's shoes as he delivered these sermons as well as sitting in the pews where these sermons were preached. He asks and addresses the hard questions I might ask.

After reading these sermons, some might say that they could have been delivered in the West as well as in the East. But the fact is that they were not preached just anywhere, but in an authoritarian country that disdained the church and the gospel. The 18th century German biblical scholar, Johannes Bengel, wrote, "Apply your whole self to the text, and the whole text to yourself." Krusche certainly heeds that advice. He preaches with a pastor's heart and sensitivity, but he also digs fiercely into the text.

I found myself moved and addressed by these sermons and hope that others will have a similar experience. This volume follows the order of the sermons that is in the original volume, that is, they are not chronological, but biblically sequential. Although one sermon is from 1977, the rest are from the decade of the 1980s. In addition to the sermons, there are also two Bible studies which he led. When Krusche refers either to hymns or other texts, I have tried to find published translations in English. When I have had to rely on my own translation, I have noted that. All the biblical texts are from the New Revised Standard Version.

My thanks go to Professor Michael Beintker, a distinguished theologian, first at the University of Halle (in East Germany) and later at the University of Münster in the West. He was the target of Stasi antics while living in Halle. His encouragement was important to this project as was that of Dr. Don McKim, a Reformed theologian and scholar in the United States.

Thanks also to my sister, Alison Meier, who was particularly helpful in working through a few difficult passages. Finally, my wife, Jo Ann, has been a constant source of support and unceasing love, and I will be forever grateful.

James S. Currie
Austin, Texas
April 2021

# Genesis 4:1-16
## September 5, 1982
### 13th Sunday after Trinity Sunday at the Cathedral in Zwickau

Now the man knew his wife Eve, and she conceived and bore Cain, saying, "I have produced a man with the help of the Lord." Next she bore his brother Abel. Now Abel was a keeper of sheep, and Cain a tiller of the ground. In the course of time Cain brought to the Lord an offering of the fruit of the ground, and Abel for his part brought of the firstlings of his flock, their fat portions. And the Lord had regard for Abel and his offering, but for Cain and his offering he had no regard. So Cain was very angry, and his countenance fell. The Lord said to Cain, "Why are you angry, and why has your countenance fallen? If you do well, will you not be accepted? And if you do not do well, sin is lurking at the door; its desire is for you, but you must master it."

Cain said to his brother Abel, "Let us go out to the field." And when they were in the field, Cain rose up against his brother Abel, and killed him. Then the Lord said to Cain, "Where is your brother Abel?" He said, "I do not know; am I my brother's keeper?" And the Lord said, "What have you done? Listen; your brother's blood is crying out to me from the ground, which has opened its mouth to receive your brother's blood from your hand. When you till the ground, it will no longer yield to you its strength; you will be a fugitive and a wanderer on the earth." Cain said to the Lord, "My punishment is greater than I can bear! Today you have driven me away from the soil, and I shall be hidden from your face; I shall be a fugitive and a wanderer on the earth, and anyone who meets me may kill me! Then the Lord said to him, "Not so! Whoever kills Cain will suffer a sevenfold vengeance." And the Lord put a mark on Cain, so that no one who came upon him would kill him. Then Cain went away from the presence of the Lord, and settled in the land of Nod, east of Eden.

Dear Friends,

Twelve years ago when I preached on this text, there appeared in Switzerland a book by an anthropologist in which there was this statement: "Cain rules the world. We point the doubter simply to the history of the world." In the meantime we have reached a point that we can no longer simply take notice. The history of the world is the story of Cain; it is the story of fratricide. If blood could cry out, which alone has been shed among us in our own story in recent months, we would not be able to bear it. We would go crazy. We are no longer as primitive as Cain. We don't kill with our own hands. We have developed techniques by which with the push of a button a few million people can be killed all at once. There are cold-blooded calculations as to how many mega-deaths result from one megaton of explosives.

How have we reached this point? Modern research into human behavior tells us of an aggressive drive with which we are born, an aggressiveness that is part of our nature, a constant readiness to oppose another or to eliminate a person. We are, so to speak, pre-programmed to be aggressive.

If then the story of humanity is inevitably Cain's story, does it also necessitate a story of fratricide? Human behaviorists reject this. They maintain that there are also other impulses, for example, the propensity for sociality and for mutual support which inhibit aggressive drives. Human behaviorists set their hope for a friendlier future on these natural opponents of aggression whose effect can be strengthened through education, culture, and change in social conditions. Sometime or other the social impulses will restrain the aggressive ones. Sometime or other. But do we still have much time? We have the impression that everything is at stake. This information is of little use.

In this enormously critical situation in which we look into the breaking up of the natural world, God wants to speak to us through this ancient story. It does not explain or excuse the fratricide with an innate aggressiveness, but rather it holds human beings inescapably responsible for their relationships and their conduct toward their neighbor. I think that through this primeval story God not only wants to hold up a mirror to us, one in which we will discover how very much we ourselves possess the characteristics we see in Cain – namely, godless, solitude, and therefore not at peace –, but also through this story we will unmistakably be made aware that God keeps watch over the brother's right to live.

1. God warns us not to lose sight of the fact that our neighbor is our sibling.

2. God refuses to permit us to ignore the matter of our relatedness.

3. God does not concede that killing our neighbor is the necessary rule of existence in the world.

I.

The conflict which ends in the demise of the brother opens with the fact that the one cannot bear how very much the other is favored over him. Abel's labor receives God's blessings, while Cain's does not. Abel has everything in abundance, while Cain is a poor wretch. For Abel everything falls into place, while nothing works for Cain. Why is this so – this glaring injustice? In the end one is not worse than the other. Cain has not worked less diligently than his brother. Has he not offered the best from the produce of his work? Indeed, Cain's offering did not require any less work than Abel's!

Why then is the one offering favored and the other disregarded, why this obvious inequality? "So Cain was very angry, and his countenance fell," we read.

I think we understand all too well how this unequal fate rankles Cain, how it boils up inside him and breaks out in jealousy. Here we recognize ourselves in him again: I have to work hard for everything while others have everything fall into their laps. Someone else's children are healthy, they flourish and become something while mine fill me only with worries and problems. The neighbor "over there" has a house and buys a new car every two years, while we drive an old clunker. They have everything while we are always standing in line. Why is that?

When such comparisons strike a chord in us, we notice that envy begins to eat away at us and takes control of us, and we are no longer able to look at our neighbor impartially, as if something stood between us. "And his countenance fell," we are told about Cain.

Whenever that happens, it is dangerous. And at that moment God warns, "Why has your countenance fallen?" Why are you no longer able to look at your brother in a gracious way? Why are you no longer able to look at him in the eye? And when you do look at him, are you aware how cold your gaze is, how you are scarcely able to conceal your hatred of him? Why do you look down? Is it because you don't want the other person to see that you no longer regard him as your brother, but rather as a stranger, an enemy? Is it because you don't want him to see what's in your heart, namely, I could kill him, this...this. Then I'll be finished with him!

"Wait a minute!" God warns. Whenever you are no longer able to see another person as your sibling, but rather as a competitor, whenever you begin to hate him or her, then you must sit up and take notice, for then "sin is lurking at the door." Be careful when spiteful thoughts rather than kind ones take hold of your heart when it appears that your neighbor is faring better than you are. "Watch out!" God warns. The murderer in you stands ready to leap whenever you no longer see others as your siblings. God warns us not to underestimate this tendency to attack our neighbor/sibling.

A final signal from the conscience: fratricide always begins when the brother does not recognize the humanity in the other person, but instead makes him into the devil. We experienced that when in the Third Reich Jews were represented as inferior parasites who sucked life out of us, and Communists as thugs who were capable of anything. It is crucial to take notice when one no longer speaks of human beings, but rather refers to them as criminal elements, mobs, or vermin. God warns us not to dehumanize our neighbor only to make it easier to do away with him or her. Be careful, do not be taken in by images that diminish others and incite hearts. It depends on you. The problem of significant differences of which there are, in fact, many between human individuals and groups can and must be resolved in ways other than by the elimination of the sibling/neighbor.

## II.

God guards the brother's right to live. God warns us not to lose sight of the fact that the other is our sibling. God refuses to permit us to ignore the matter of our relatedness.

Cain's deed takes place outside where there are no witnesses. And the story tells us that everyone is capable of that, even those who present gifts to God. We are capable of that as well.

No one saw what happened there and how it happened. Perhaps Cain removed all traces of evidence and buried his dead brother. Perhaps he thought that now he was rid of him and he could go on his merry way. The competitor was eliminated, the favored one was removed, and with the outrageous injustice. Now there was only an open road.

But that is the great mistake. God guards the brother's right to live. Whoever lays hands on a sibling's life must answer to God. God's question is no longer the one addressed to Adam, "Where are you?" but rather, "Where is your brother?" The individual is no longer responsible only for himself, but also now for the sibling. "Where is your brother? What have you done?" No one can dodge this question.

And neither can we. I believe this question frightens and stings you as much as it does me. Where is your brother? Spit it out! Where is he – where are the six million Jews whom you Germans killed in the so-called Third Reich? What have you done? Are there among us those who at the time as Hitler Youth or S.A. people cried out, "Kill the Jew!"? Where is your brother Abel? What about the 15 million children whom you starve every year of hunger because you think that money can be better used for more important things – like armaments. We kill with weapons before they are used and even if they are never used. Where is your brother Abel? And what of those malaria victims whom you let die because the money in the world that is spent a half a day on military issues and which would be enough to eradicate this horrible illness – because this money is used for armaments instead? Where is your brother Abel? What of those who are murdered in Chile, Argentina, and Ethiopia? And what of the hundreds of millions who still live, but whose deaths have long since been figured into the planning of atomic strategies?

Cain tried to escape the grasp of the question about his brother by posing an impudent question, "Am I my brother's keeper?" Am I my brother's baby-sitter? He can very well look after himself! But it is not such a simple thing to slither away from responsibility. God dismisses his excuses: "What have you done? Your brother's blood is crying out to me from the ground!"

We are responsible for the life of our brother. And life today is threatened as never before in history. Do we want to escape responsibility and declare that we have no influence and can change nothing? Suppose one were to counter with: I will not cooperate, I will not touch any weapon. That is not a solution to the problem, but a passive sign of responsibility. Should not Christians the world over declare, We do not want to be protected by atomic weapons. We renounce this kind of protection. For us it makes no sense to justify defense by employing atomic weapons and thereby threatening the painful death of millions of defenseless human beings.

Whoever does not want to be his brother's keeper becomes his brother's murderer. In today's Gospel lesson (Luke 10:25-37) the priest and the Levite, who leave responsibility for the dying man to others, are no better than Cain.

God guards the brother's right to life. God hears the cries of those in Chile, Argentina, Iran, and Ethiopia who have been swept aside, even when everything has gone silent and there are no human witnesses aside from the murderers. God hears the cries from the torture chambers, the cages in which persons are imprisoned and tortured to death. The cries of mothers in Beirut. No cry fades away unheard. There is one who hears them.

And God not only hears. Whoever thinks that, when the last opponent is eliminated, he can finally live undisturbed and in peace, is terribly mistaken. "Listen; your brother's blood is crying out to me from the ground! And now you are cursed from the ground.... You will be a fugitive and a wanderer on the earth," God says to the brother murderer. You can no longer hide. Whoever has his brother on his conscience must bear the curse of vulnerability and of being an outcast, of wandering aimlessly. With that comes fear. Because we know our thoughts about the brother, we do not need to imagine his thoughts about us. That is most unsettling. Who then knows if one day someone might not do what we are only thinking? Fear of another, mistrust, suspicions, spying, informing, disguising. "You will be a fugitive and a wanderer on the earth." It is truly unbearable. Then Cain said to God, "My punishment is greater than I can bear."

III.

God guards the brother's right to live. God refuses to let us ignore the matter of our sibling. God does not allow fratricide to become the norm of our world.

The last word in this story of the brother-less person is not the bottomless pit of despair over his unbearable situation, but rather the last word is God's unfathomable mercy. "So it will be that anyone who meets me may kill me," says the frightened murderer. "Then the Lord said to him, 'Not so! Whoever kills Cain will suffer a sevenfold vengeance.' And the Lord put a mark on Cain, so that no one who came upon him would kill him." Both in spite of and with his guilt he is allowed to continue to live. The murder of his brother should not become the norm of human existence. It should not be the norm to seek vengeance.

That is the case because this story continues. It ends where the Son of God becomes Cain's brother. His brothers kill him and bring on themselves the righteous blood that is shed on the earth, from the innocent blood of Abel – as it is described in the Passion story. But he, the Son of God and our brother, prayed for his murderers from the cross, "Father, forgive them!" Our help in answering the question, "Where is your brother?" is found in pointing to the cross. There is my brother. He died both because of me and for me. The voice of the blood of my brother who was hung on the cross by me and for me cries to God – but not against me but for me. In Hebrews we read, "and to Jesus, the mediator of a new covenant, and to the sprinkled blood that speaks a better word than the blood of Abel" (Heb. 12:24).

And now our story need no longer be the story of Cain. Since Christ, our brother, died by our hands and for us, Cain is no longer our inevitable lot. The path is released to the community of the Crucified one to establish human relationships in a new way. In and with the church of Jesus Christ God has begun the story of fellowship in the midst of this fratricidal world. In this fellowship we find what John describes: "For this is the message you have heard from the beginning, that we should love one another. We must not be like Cain who was from the evil one and murdered his brother.... We know that we have passed from death to life because we love one another" (I John 3:11ff., 14).

We must be Cain no longer. No more do we need to cast our eyes into the darkness. We may once again look to God and thereby see others as our brothers and sisters. No one can now make others enemies whom we need to hate and destroy. For us that is true, once and for all. We are poor victors. We have been brought from death to life and can now love our brothers and sisters. Amen.

# Genesis 22:1-14
## September 18, 1988
### 16th Sunday after Trinity Sunday at St. Peter's Church, Copenhagen, Denmark

After these things God tested Abraham. He said to him, "Abraham!" And he said, "Here I am." He said, "Take your son, your only son Isaac, whom you love, and go to the land of Moriah, and offer him there as a burnt offering on one of the mountains that I shall show you." So Abraham rose early in the morning, saddled his donkey, and took two of his young men with him, and his son Isaac; he cut the wood for the burnt offering, and set out and went to the place in the distance that God had shown him. On the third day Abraham looked up and saw the place far away. Then Abraham said to his young men, "Stay here with the donkey; the boy and I will go over there; we will worship, and then we will come back to you." Abraham took the wood of the burnt offering and laid it on his son Isaac, and he himself carried the fire and the knife. So the two of them walked on together. Isaac said to his father Abraham, "Father!" And he said, "Here I am, my son." He said, "The fire and the wood are here, but where is the lamb for a burnt offering?" Abraham said, "God himself will provide the lamb for a burnt offering, my son." So the two of them walked on together.

When they came to the place that God had shown him, Abraham built an altar there and laid the wood in order. He bound his son Isaac, and laid him on the altar, on top of the wood. Then Abraham reached out his hand and took the knife to kill his son. But the angel of the Lord called to him heaven, and said, "Abraham! Abraham!" And he said, "Here I am." He said, "Do not lay your hand on the boy or do anything to him; for now I know that you fear God, since you have not withheld your son, your only son, from me." And Abraham looked up and saw a ram, caught in a thicket by its horns. Abraham went and took the ram and offered it up as a burnt offering instead of his son. So Abraham called that place "The Lord will provide"; as it is said to this day, "On the mount of the Lord it shall be provided."

Dear Friends, I know there are those who are shocked at what God expects of Abraham here. To sacrifice one's own child seems inhuman to us. We wince at the thought. It is impossible to demand that. Strangely, we do not react nearly as indignantly when we consider the expectation that each state has of its citizens that they sacrifice their own sons for their country. And we do not react so sensitively when a man demands that a young girl offer their child to a good calling or career, and to do so when it is still in the womb. Whether the sacrifice occurs by one's own hand – as with Abraham – or by the hand of another is perhaps a slight distinction. This variation in reaction is a bit peculiar.

Be that as it may, in this story no child is killed at all. While we know the story as "The Sacrifice of Isaac", the fact is that it's the story of the non-sacrifice. Abraham is not commanded, "Kill your child!" but rather "Bring your child as a sacrifice to God!" Not "Lay your hand on your child!" but "Place your child in God's hand!" And that is something quite different. In addition, the story is not simply about a child. There is another, deeper level to the story.

Most of us are somewhat familiar with Abraham. God had commanded him to leave home, health, security, and all that was reliable, and to enter a completely open future that was new, strange, and full of uncertainty: "Go from your country and your kindred and your father's house to the land that I will show you." And with that command God had made a promise: "I will make of you a great nation and I will bless you, and make your name great, so that you will be a blessing.... In you all the families of the earth shall be blessed" (Gen. 12:1-3).

Abraham – the blessing-bearer for the world. Everything good and healthy that God had intended for humankind was to come into the world through him and his posterity. All that Abraham took with him when he departed was his faith – his faith that God keeps God's promises. But this promise does not appear to be kept. Abraham remained childless. How was he to become a great nation without a son? Even when he and Sarah were beyond child-bearing years, he held fast to the promise. It would have been understandable for him to give up, to be resigned to the possibility that it was perhaps not God's will for which he had waited with such hope and joy. He did not lose hope, but rather he persisted in believing that, in spite of doubts in his own heart, God would be true to his word. And God was. Against all human expectation it happened: Isaac was born. The son, the visible guarantor that as the blessing-bearer for the world there would be a great nation. On him, the only son, everything depended – the whole meaning of Abraham's story heretofore: his obedient departure from everything having to do with an earlier life in Uz, on him hung the guarantee of the future story of God's blessing for the world. Quite simply, everything stood or fell with Isaac. With this son the circumstances are unique.

The command: "Take your son, your only son Isaac, whom you love, and go to the land of Moriah, and offer him there as a burnt offering!" – this command annuls and cancels everything if Isaac had to be sacrificed, then the sacrifice of leaving home country and friends was in vain, and Abraham's faith and anticipation that he would hold a son in his arms were futile. Seventy years of unflinching expectation, the joy at the realization of faith, all in vain. There would be no true nation that bore God's blessing, God's salvation brought into the world. God appeared to have opposed his own promise and abrogated it. Believe it or not.

We don't know what may have been in Abraham's heart when he received this command. With a bit of psychology we can imagine a rather tense internal struggle. The story mentions nothing of this. We hear only Abraham's response to God's call: "Here am I", and that he listened silently. He did not dispute whether or not God had the right to demand this from him. He does not say, "Demand what you will! Do with me whatever you like. Take me as a sacrifice, take my life, take all that I have, but leave my son alone!" "Take my body, by possessions, my honor, but not my wife and child!" God may not do that. Abraham did not count on God prescribing how far he might go, where it would begin to become inhuman, how much danger would be involved, so much so that one would not be able to distinguish him from a demon. Abraham did not for a moment question God's claim on us. By no means did he grasp it. That, too, is incomprehensible. But Abraham opted for the dark and difficult path of obedience in faith. The narrator indicates how difficult it was by Abraham's silence. In oppressive silence Abraham and Isaac walk on.

We are told that Abraham left behind those who had accompanied them. Ancient biblical interpreters suggested that he did this because he must have been afraid that they would try to dissuade him from the path of obedience, that they would stand in his way, that they would cry out against him because it was impossible that God would demand such a thing. Who knows what he heard? In any case, he did not hear God's voice. They would prevent the sacrifice of a boy at the whim of an old man.

I think that on the long journey Abraham had to have constantly struggled within his own heart. Was he sure that it was God who had commanded him to sacrifice Isaac? Should he not instead turn back and say to God, I cannot do this. I'm simply not ready. Should he not ask God to demand something else from him – his life, but not that of the boy. But then Abraham would not have become the father of faith, the blessing-bearer for the world. He stays prepared to offer everything – himself, his son, and with the guarantor for the redemptive future of the world.

I have already mentioned that the demand of Abraham is unique, not to be compared with any other to the extent that it was the demand to give up his only son, but also the bearer of the promised blessing for the world. The demand is singular. But the question that God poses to Abraham – he also poses to us. Are you prepared to give up that on which your life depends, that which is most important to you, that by means of which you see your future guaranteed? Are you prepared to give up plans for your life if I were to demand that of you? Are you prepared to sacrifice what's most important to you, what you think is yours; to let go or give up, to renounce whatever stands or falls for you? Will you place yourself completely at my disposal?

When I was still a bishop, a young theology student came to me one day with his girlfriend. She was from West Germany. He had fallen in love with her and wanted to marry her, but she did not want to live in East Germany. Her mother especially did not want that. Her daughter could not live in East Germany. If the young man wanted to marry her daughter, he would have to move to West Germany. He could preach God's Word there. He asked me if he should try to emigrate. I told him that God needed him here (in East Germany)! And he sacrificed his love to God. It couldn't be more costly. The God of Abraham is not a God for the bourgeoisie. God asks, To which obedience does your faith belong? That sounds harsh, as harsh as Jesus' word: "Whoever loves son or daughter more than me is not worthy of me" (Mt. 10:37b).

But the God with whom Abraham is dealing, the Father of Jesus Christ, is not a heartless God who demands ice-cold obedience. God does not demand military-like obedience which deals with bodies and, when necessary, with the bodies of blood relatives. Only the devil demands such obedience.

The question God poses to Abraham and to us is not simply, Are you prepared for the most extreme obedience? That is part of the other question, Are you prepared to trust me to the end? Are you ready to let go of everything that has to do with your future because you trust that your future is in my hands? Or, even plainer, will you obey me completely because you rely wholly on my word, because you absolutely trust my promise?

There are two points of curiosity in our story. When Abraham leaves his friends behind, he says to them, "Stay here with the donkey. The boy and I will go over there; we will worship, and then we will come back to you." Was that not an untruthful evasion? Abraham knew that he would not be returning with the boy, but rather he would be coming back alone. I think this statement was not intentionally deceitful, but rather it resonates with hope. Even if I return without my son because I have given him up to God, I will not be returning alone, not as a fraud, not as one who has lost faith in God's promises and sees in them only empty words. I don't know how this will play out – it does not look hopeful – but God will not let me take the difficult road back alone.

The second point of curiosity is even more noteworthy. After the friends are left behind, Abraham and Isaac continue walking in silence. Not a word passes between them. The father carries the knife and the fire, the dangerous items which could cause harm to the boy who carries the wood. And then the boy breaks the oppressive silence and asks the father, "The fire and the wood are here, but where is the lamb for a burnt offering?" "My son," the father replies, "God himself will provide the lamb for a burnt offering." And because the answer came from the father, Isaac was satisfied. But was that not again an evasive, embarrassing response? Abraham knew whom God had chosen for the burn offering. Not a lamb, but the boy who walked trustingly beside him. That God would show him a ram was known to the narrator of the story who had said at the very outset that God wanted to put Abraham to the test. But Abraham did not know this; otherwise, the test of his faithful obedience could have been a pure pretense. No, for him it was deadly serious. With his answer surely Abraham wanted to spare the boy. But there is more to his answer, namely, if the son dies by my hand, then he dies into the hand of the living God, into the hand that will never let him die.

In a sermon Martin Luther said the following about this story: "Both had to be true. Abraham believed and knew nothing but that his son had to die. And at the same time that he was to become the father of many nations. How does this make any sense? He had to be thinking, God is omnipotent and all-knowing. Today I still have a son, but tomorrow I will have nothing but ashes. But God can do so much. If I and the whole world were dead, God could wake him up, even after 100 years, and make him a father. So, God grants him (Abraham) no more than the single comfort to which he clings, that God would bring him (Isaac) back to life when he wants to because God doesn't lie."[1]

Abraham does not say, God won't do it or God cannot do it, but rather, I see nothing at all. Everything is completely dark. But God sees through the darkness – "and Abraham called that place 'The Lord will provide'" as we read at the end of the story. And where I can no longer see anything, God sees how things will turn out. I know nothing, only that God does not deceive and that God makes good on his promises. Even when God expects me to bury my hope – he stands at the graveside of my hope, the living God, the one who raises the dead. Even if I must let go of my life's plans, God has a life prepared for me.

In the letter to the Hebrews we read in the chapter on the roll call of the faithful in the Old Testament, "By faith Abraham, when put to the test, offered up Isaac. He who had received the promises was ready to offer up his only son.... He considered the fact that

---

[1] Translator's note: This is my translation.

God is able even to raise someone from the dead" (Heb. 11:17, 19).

God required of Abraham that he travel the dark path of faith obedience. But God spared both Abraham and Isaac. On Mount Moriah God deflected the supreme human sacrifice in order to sacrifice himself on Golgotha for our salvation. God spared Abraham and his son, but did not spare his only Son, but gave him up to death for us all, and raised him for us all, so that we might live through him. God, you "gave your dearest treasure."[2]

We belong to the God of Abraham, Isaac, and Jacob, the Father of Jesus Christ. He wants only one thing from us, namely, that we entrust ourselves to him and walk the path of faith which is no longer confusing, but remains certain: Whatever God requires of me, I will put my life and future in his hands – in the hands of the one who said, "No one will snatch them out of my hand" (John 10:28b). Amen.

---

[2] Translator's note: This is from the fourth stanza of the German hymn by Martin Luther, "Nun freut euch, lieben Christen g'mein". The English is "Dear Christians, One and All, Rejoice" and can be found in the Evangelical Lutheran hymnal, Worship (Hymn #594).

# Genesis 28:10-19a
## September 4, 1983
14th Sunday after Trinity Sunday in the Cathedral in Magdeburg

Jacob left Beersheba and went toward Haran. He came to a certain place and stayed for the night, because the sun had set. Taking one of the stones of the place, he put it under his head and lay down in that place. And he dreamed that there was a ladder set up on the earth, the top of it reaching to heaven; and the angels of God were ascending and descending on it. And the Lord stood beside him and said, "I am the Lord, the God of Isaac; the land on which you lie I will give to you and to your offspring; and your offspring shall be like the dust of the earth, and you shall spread abroad to the west and to the east and to the north and to the south; and all the families of the earth shall be blessed in you and in your offspring. Know that I am with you and will keep you wherever you go, and will bring you back to this land; for I will not leave you until I have done what I have promised you." Then Jacob woke from his sleep and said, "Surely the Lord is in this place – and I did not know it!" And he was afraid, and said, "How awesome is this place! This is none other than the house of God, and this is the gate of heaven."

So Jacob rose early in the morning, and he took the stone that he had put under his head and set it up for a pillar and poured oil on the top of it. He called that place Bethel.

Dear Friends! In this worship service we will deal with the God of Jacob, whom we confess as the Father of Jesus Christ. This story concerns us because from it something will open up for us in this service, namely,

1. God encounters us when and where God wills.

2. God bridges the distance between God and us.

3. God accompanies us and brings us to the goal.

## I.

Jacob most definitely did not seek out this encounter with God. He is fleeing from an unsettled past. And so one tries to get out of God's way. Someone with an unsettled past has no interest in praying or in worship. We know Jacob's past. He cheated his brother in an evil way and thus shattered that relationship. And that's why he had become anxious. Who knows what takes place in the heart of the embittered brother? Perhaps it is better to stay out of sight. He who does not restore a relationship that he is guilty of breaking and tries to escape this unsettled past in order to be free of it, in reality he takes it with him into an unfathomable and fearful future. And precisely there, fleeing from a confused past into an uncertain future, that is where Jacob runs into the unexpected presence of God – as night falls, in a desert, under the open skies, when he is dead tired.

God has his time and place, God sets the when and the where as he allows human beings to experience his presence. Jacob neither sought nor desired nor expected this encounter. He also cannot escape it. I can imagine that there are some here who would be able to share a time in their life when God encountered them in an unsought, unrequested, surprising way. In this story the most surprising thing for me is that God does not stop this man who is fleeing and say, "Stop! Where are you going? What have you done to your brother – and to your aging father? Do you think you can simply run away from them?" But there's none of that. The matter of guilt is surprisingly not raised. God can encounter people in completely other ways. "Adam, where are you?" God asks the one who thinks he can hide from and outlast God. "Where is your brother Abel?" he asks the one who attacked his brother.

It's different here. God does not act with intrigue. He meets when, where, and how he wishes. It is always unique. Because of that, no one may normalize how persons have experienced God or how God has encountered them.

If the ancients had built a place of worship here – a Bethel – and told this story to those who came – you did not meet just anywhere, but rather it was here that you encountered the God of Jacob in an unforgettable way, then they naturally knew of this freedom of God. They knew that God cannot be confined. They were not so primitive as to think that God lives in this house as we live in houses, this God whom all in heaven cannot grasp. But they also knew that God could be found in this house, that here they could be drawn into the story that began here, the story of promise and blessing.

Of course, we enlightened Protestants certainly know that God is not bound to sacred places and sacred times. From that, many have concluded that they do not need sacred places. They can even cite Luther who said, "Wherever God's Word is heard, be it in the forest or in the water or wherever, there is a Bethel." While that is certainly so, I have rarely heard God's Word in the forest or in the water.

Certainly God meets people not only in houses of worship which we have built and in worship services which we hold. But here God wants to meet us, here we may most certainly await God where we are gathered as a community and hear God's Word and celebrate the Lord's Supper. Without these concrete places and times we would have long ago lost God, and our own notions would have come to nought.

In the 15 years that I have served here as preacher and bishop this house of worship, this cathedral, has become dear to me for all the ways that I have experienced and have been blessed by the living God in this congregation. Some experiences have been profound and, for me, unforgettable. The heavens have opened up for us. Thus, communities justifiably maintain their churches.

It is true that God meets us whenever and wherever God wills. God does not need a specific place or time. But we need them. I am happy that we have them. Here God's Word can be heard and the table set. This is reflected in one of our Advent hymns: "Behold, how very pleasant it is to call that place that we find the one whom we meet in Communion, baptism, and Word." This cathedral has become a most pleasant place for me and, no doubt, for many of you as well.

## II.

The second thing that unfolds from this story from God is this: God bridges the distance between God and us.

Jacob lies down and has a dream. Here again it becomes clear how free God is. God is not at our beck and call; we cannot prescribe time and place for God. God simply comes. God encounters a person – unsought, unexpected, and even irresistible. The dream that is dreamt here is neither a wish-fulfillment nor a nightmare, but it is a memorable dream.

The ladder that appears in the dream is not set up on the earth to reach the heavens, but rather is aimed towards the earth. Jacob who is sleeping on the ground dreams not of climbing the ladder towards heaven, but instead heaven comes down to him. The ladder connects, so to speak, the place where God dwells with the place God will appear. No human being can be seen on the ladder. The ladder offers no place for human beings who always want to go beyond themselves, and yet never reach heaven, and thus always end up by themselves.

The ladder is reserved for angels whose movement always starts in heaven. Through them God reveals God's self to human beings, bridging the infinite distance – not spatially, but the distance between God and sinners – God creates the possibility of an encounter. The image of the heavenly ladder is the counter image of the story of the tower of Babel. There human beings make the futile attempt to establish contact with heaven, while here the contact comes from God. We cannot reach God, but God can come to us. We do not live under a closed heaven, but an open one.

Long before the birth of Christ, the heavenly ladder to the God who wants to come to human beings describes the Advent-ful incarnational God. This is the God who could be God without us, but who does not want to be without us. And after contact is made – in the birth of Christ – Jesus takes up this illustration and says about himself, "You will see heaven opened and the angels of God ascending and descending upon the Son of Man" (John 1:51). He is our Bethel. In him God meets us. "For in him the whole fullness of deity dwells bodily," we read in Colossians (2:9).

Whoever comes into contact with Jesus comes into contact with the power-filled blessing of the divine realm. Whoever is in touch with Jesus, above whom heaven is open, no longer lives under the lock and key of a future-less world and no longer must dream from this world in order to come to oneself, but now stands in the wide space of the promise. That person no longer sees oneself hopelessly abandoned, but rather knows that God is present in it and has begun God's story of blessing in which everyone has a part. With that we come to the third point that is evident in this story of the God of Jacob.

## III.

God accompanies us and brings us to the goal.

God comes to Jacob not only in a silent dream, but God addresses him personally: "I am the Lord, the God of Abraham your father and the God of Isaac; the land on which you lie I will give to you and to your offspring.... Know that I am with you and will keep you wherever you go, and will bring you back to this land; for I will not leave you until I have done what I have promised you."

Jacob must go on. One can stay in God's house only for a short time. Jacob must continue his long, long journey on which in the morning he would not know where he would be in the evening. He had no idea what kind of path lay ahead, what kind of grandiose detour might lie ahead. First, there's the flight over the border to relatives in Mesopotamia. Twenty years of hard labor there. Seven years of waiting for the promised Rachel and cheated into having Leah, and again defrauded of agreed upon wages, then escaping under cover of darkness with his family and all his property, back to his home country, along the way fearful of encountering the brother he had deceived, the mysterious disappearance of his son Joseph, the death of his beloved wife, famine in the land, the painful trek to Egypt, his life as an old man in a foreign country, and finally not being buried in his own homeland.

What do we know of our own path? You young people – where will you be in ten or twenty years? What will you experience in the meantime? Will the world look a little brighter for you than it does now? Will there be hills and valleys or dead-ends and detours? And we old folks? What will the final leg of our journey look like? What will we face?

Jacob had to go through uncertain times, but with all the uncertainty there was a final certainty, namely, he traveled with God's promise: "I am the Lord, the God of Abraham your father and the God of Isaac.... I am with you and will keep you wherever you go, and will bring you back to this land." We don't need any more than that. The God on whom our fathers and mothers depended also goes with us. We have a God who not only knows our path, but who also walks with us. The God who accompanies. The God who is not attached to some holy place, but who travels with us. The solid place where God encounters us, and the wide path on which God accompanies us – Bethel and Mesopotamia, the cathedral and our everyday paths – belong together. And, above all, our paths stand under the promise that they will lead home. "I am with you...and will bring you back to this land," God said to Jacob. And Jesus tells us, "And remember, I am with you always, to the end of the age" (Mt. 28:20b), "and where I am, there will my servant be also" (John 12:26a), "when I am lifted up from the earth, I will draw all people to myself" (John 12:32).

The story of God's promise to God's people runs to the eternal home, to the future city to which all our wanderings and flights, stretches of thirst and happiness, our detours and wrong-headed paths lead, and in which God will live with God's people forever. All our life's paths are paths home. With this promise we can sing: "I walk along the road that leads home because my Father comforts me without conditions."[3] Amen.

---

[3] Translator's note: From Paul Gerhardt's hymn "Ich bin ein Gast auf Erden" (stanza 6). My translation.

# Exodus 20:2a & 3
## March 27, 1983
Palm Sunday at the Salvator Church in Prague on the 500th anniversary of Martin Luther's Birth

I am the Lord your God: you shall have no other gods before me.

The grace of our Lord Jesus Christ and the love of God and the fellowship of the Holy Spirit be with you all!

Dear brothers and sisters! I am delighted to share in this worship service with you. We thank God for the spiritual riches which God has given us through his witness, Martin Luther. I serve as bishop of the church in the region of which the most important places of his life and work are located: Eisleben, the city of his birth 500 years ago, Erfurt, Wittenberg, Torgau. I bring heartfelt greetings from there and from the Protestant church in the GDR as a whole. You are our dear friends.

Martin Luther had a warm relationship with the Bohemian brothers. After various initial misunderstandings about deeply held convictions, they agreed essentially to a unity, so that in 1538 Luther could write, We who were once far apart have come closer to each other and are like one flock led by one shepherd.

Your church has surely benefited from Luther's theological ideas and spiritual insights, and has exhibited them in its life; otherwise, you would have no cause to remember him with gratitude before God. In the years that followed, on the other hand, we have been enriched by your spiritual contributions. In our hymnbook there are twenty hymns from your hymnal. And this benefit has continued into the present. The names Hromadka, Soucek, and Dobias cannot be forgotten by many of us.[4] Members of your

---

[4]Translator's note: Joseph Hromadka (1889-1969), Josef Soucek (1864-1938), and Frantisek Dobias (1907-1972) are all Czech theologians.

Comenius University faculty have taught at our universities, delegates from your church have attended our Synod meetings, and the kind of courageous faith you have shown as disciples of the Crucified one has deeply moved and encouraged us. That I am permitted to preach in this service of worship is for me evidence of the spiritual exchange that is vitally necessary for the church as the body of Christ.

As the theme for this Luther anniversary year the Protestant churches in the GDR have chosen the interpretation of the first commandment that Luther offered in the Small Catechism.

"I am the Lord your God. You shall have no other gods before me" is the first commandment. And here is Luther's comment: "We should fear, love, and trust in God above all things."[5] "I am," says God; "we should," says Luther. From God's exhortation Luther hears immediately God's total claim on us. There is no part of our life – neither our intimate, personal life nor our public, political life – that does not concern God, and in which we could free ourselves from God, and in which we are not responsible to God. We are always in God's presence, always in God's field of vision.

It would be dreadful if God were like the spy who has eyes and ears everywhere in order to keep human beings in fear and under control. We could neither love nor trust such a God. But God is no spy. The eyes which are directed at us are not cold and suspicious, but gaze at us lovingly. "I am the Lord your God" is not spoken by a distrusting tyrant, but rather by the God who has revealed his heart in Jesus Christ. In one of his sermons Luther said, "God is a burning oven full of love which spans from the earth to heaven."

Not some kind of "higher being", this God who out of compassion gave us his beloved son in the death of a sinner – in our place, for us, on our behalf – this God of the Passion with the wounds of the cross, this God we are "above all things to fear, love, and trust."

---

[5] Luther's Small Catechism, "The First Commandment".

## I.

We begin with love. "To love God above all things" – what does that mean for me, personally? I believe, above all, it means this: I depend on God's Yes that God never revokes. I believe in God's love and I entrust myself to it. I know that God loves me, a sinner, completely floundering unless God comes to me. As Luther says in the Heidelberg Disputation, God's love is not for the lovable, but rather it is self-creating. And in another place, "Sinners are beautiful because they are loved. They are not loved because they are beautiful."[6]

To love God above all else means: for this completely undeserved gift of love to respond to God with mutual love, to reflect God's love to God and to reflect that love to others with gratitude and service. He gave "your dearest treasure," sings Luther.[7] Thus, I want to so love God with gratitude and service, so that I won't have to ask, Would less be enough? God has given his very best, and now my love cannot be any less. It may cost me my heart's desire. It may cost me the cross.

## II.

And now to trust. "We should love and trust God above all things.

What does that mean for the church if it totally and completely puts its trust in God? Negatively, it will not place its confidence in human beings, in good relationships, in a few influential people, in its skillful diplomacy. We read in the Psalms: "It is better to take refuge in the Lord than to put confidence in mortals." "Do not put your trust in princes, in mortals, in whom there is no help" (118:8; 146:3). Thus, we place our trust in God's promises and not in the promises of others. God is true to whatever God promises. "God cannot lie," Luther impresses on us over and over again. When the

---

[6] Translator's note: Heidelberg Disputation #28.
[7] Translator's note: Last line of verse 4 of "Dear Christians, One and All, Rejoice" – #594 in the Evangelical Lutheran hymnal Worship; the German text is from the hymn "Nun freut euch, lieben Christen g'mein".

Lord promised, "I am with you always, to the end of the age" (Mt. 28:20b), that is so. My brothers and sisters, you may and should depend on that. God is with you with a strength that is powerful among the weak, with the Spirit which takes your fears away and frees you to make the bold confession: "the Spirit and the gifts are ours through him who with us sideth" sang Martin Luther.[8]

And when the Lord promises, "The gates of hell will not prevail against my church" (Mt. 16:18b), then you may and should fully rely on that. You will remain and be God's witnesses. Ultimately, you are unassailable. "A mighty fortress is our God, a bulwark never failing." You belong to a God on whom you may depend, a God with whom you are safe. Thus, the elders in the brotherhood in Bohemia and Moravia expressed their experience in a letter to Luther in 1536: "Neither we nor our ancestors ever attributed the power to save us to assistance from living or dead saints, to our works or to those of others, or anything else, but rather wholly and exclusively to our own and the eternal God – Father, Son, and Holy Spirit. He alone is our goal and foundation (from him we seek favor and grace), we call upon him, all our trust is in him."

That is a marvelous confession from your parents in the faith. A church that trusts in God alone and above all else will always be a church that prays. In prayer it entrusts itself and all things to God and expects all things from God. "Trust God above all else" always means trusting God above all disappointments and in all times of suffering, clinging to God when times are difficult, when human counsel is at an end and we are at our wit's end. Whoever trusts God above all else entrusts himself or herself to the one who raises the dead and believes that God bears us over the abyss and does not let us fall into it, that one who gives us the very best, even that which we cannot imagine.

---

[8] Translator's note: From the 4th stanza of Luther's hymn "A Mighty Fortress Is Our God".

## III.

For Luther the first commandment also means that we are to fear God above all else. That means that we must always be on guard for what real life may bring us. We take quite seriously that we stand under God's No whenever we do not let God be God, whenever we do not honor God and thus do not believe that God loves us unconditionally, whenever we do not trust God, but instead seek help elsewhere and use God as a stopgap, whenever we ask God for less than what God wants to give us. At that point God turns away from us and leaves us to ourselves. To be left to ourselves – our wishes, our desires, our fears – that is hell. "Fear him who can destroy both soul and body in hell" (Mt. 10:28b), Jesus says. I fear nothing more than that God might leave me to my own devices and that God might leave the church to its own devices. We would then be lost.

To fear God above all else means to love God first with gratitude and service, to trust God with our whole heart, and to cling to God and his Word, and to be led by God. Whoever fears God above all else naturally fears God more than human beings who can only kill the body but cannot hurt the soul, the life connection to God.

To fear, love, and trust God above all else – therein lies human freedom. Amen.

# Numbers 11:4-6, 11-17, 24-29
## May 22, 1983
### Pentecost at the Cathedral in Magdeburg

The rabble among them had a strong craving; and the Israelites also wept again, and said, "If only we had meat to eat! We remember the fish we used to eat in Egypt for nothing, the cucumbers, the melons, the leeks, the onions, and the garlic; but now our strength is dried up, and there is nothing at all but this manna to look at."

So Moses said to the Lord, "Why have you treated your servant so badly? Why have I not found favor in your sight, that you lay the burden of all this people on me? Did I conceive all this people? Did I give birth to them, that you should say to me, 'Carry them in your bosom, as a nurse carries a sucking child' to the land that you promised on oath to their ancestors? Where am I to get meat to give all this people? For they come weeping to me and say, 'Give us meat to eat!' I am not able to carry all this people alone, for they are too heavy for me. If this is the way you are going to treat me, put me to death at once – if I have found favor in your sight – and do not let me see my misery."

So the Lord said to Moses, "Gather for me seventy of the elders of Israel, whom you know to be the elders of the people and officers over them; bring them to the tent of meeting, and have them take their place there with you. I will come down and talk with you there; and I will take some of the spirit that is on you and put it on them; and they shall bear the burden of the people along with you so that you will not bear all by yourself."

So Moses went out and told the people the words of the Lord; and he gathered seventy elders of the people, and placed them all around the tent. Then the Lord came down in the cloud and spoke to him, and took some of the spirit that was on him and put it on the seventy elders; and when the spirit rested upon them, they prophesied. But they did not do so again.

Two men remained in the camp, one named Eldad, and the other Medad, and the spirit rested on them; they were among those registered, but they had not gone out to the tent, and so they prophesied in the camp. And a young man ran and told Moses, "Eldad and Medad are prophesying in the camp." And Joshua son of Nun, the assistant of Moses, one of his chosen men, said, "My lord Moses, stop them!" But Moses said to him, "Are you jealous for my sake? Would that all the Lord's people were prophets, and that the Lord would put his spirit on them!"

Dear Friends! A Pentecost story from the Old Testament. Though an ancient story, it preserves in it lively experiences which are eager to be re-told because they occur in fresh ways.

What is presented as a Pentecost experience can be summarized succinctly: God's Spirit stirs up the church again.

1. God intervenes in bleak situations.

2. God abolishes the one-man system.

3. God inspires fresh beginnings.

## I.

Those who report this experience are honest about confessing openly that things looked to be lousy at the time for the people of God. With great excitement they had risked the exodus, the departure from slavery into freedom, the trek from coercion into freedom, from a foreign country into a land promised to them. But the excitement had not lasted long. They had not counted on the possibility that the path to freedom might mean serious hardships. What they experienced there was not the kind of freedom they had in mind, namely, the freedom that went according to their taste.

To be continually eating manna which God gave them was not satisfactory. They had forgotten that without this gift from heaven they would have died. Always the same. To be sure, it was filling, but now they had had enough. Now they had to have meat. If we don't have meat immediately, the whole matter of freedom is over. If there is not meat – why did we really leave Egypt? Sure, servitude was not pleasant, but at least we had fish, and as much as we wanted, and it was even free. And add to that cucumbers, melons, and onions! It was enough to make their mouth water. But this we know: when the present looks gray, the past looks golden.

It could not be clearer what misery motivated their exodus. Their whole heart was not in their departure nor were they aware of the consequences. At least with their bellies they were still in Egypt. Whatever interest they had was defined by their memory. They never really left Egypt behind them, and thus remained prisoners of their past. Wandering in the prison of the past, they have no future. Dissatisfied, pouty, sulky, full of self-pity, always glancing backward, they moved dully on. A wretched crowd having completely forgotten what God had done for them.

And Moses, called by God and charged with leading the people of God, was fed up. Always the same old song – the lifeless comparison with the golden past in which at least their existence was assured; the desire for a freedom which God directs according to their liking; the rebuke of Moses for the duration of this trek and that he had misled them. Moses neither can nor wants to bear this any longer. He lays all this before God and accuses God: "How can you demand of me that I carry this people on my arms to the land that you promised on oath to their ancestors?" "I am not able to carry all this people alone, for they are too heavy for me. If this is the way you are going to treat me, put me to death at once." One could hardly have more clearly thrown in the towel! God, if you cannot do your work any better than this, then please spare me such a futile life!

Into this bleak situation of the people of God breaks the Spirit of Pentecost which changes it. That should be pursued further as experience: Even when the community believes it has no future, when it won't let go of its past, when nothing more can be said of a sense of community life, then one must not believe that it is the end, but rather one must wait for the miracle of the Spirit of God that awakens life.

## II.

God's Spirit stirs up the church again. It breaks in in desperate situations. It ends the one-man system. Moses is so overwhelmed because he thinks he alone must bear the whole burden of responsibility. God gave him his marching orders, and now he must do everything himself. Evidently, it is inconceivable to him that there could be others besides him among the people of God who might be capable of sharing responsibility. Laypeople as well as some pastors know this: they lament endlessly about how overburdened they are, but they are not prepared to share their work. Somehow they seem to think that God has assigned first and last responsibility to them and that only they can carry it out. But it is not simply that they don't want to share the work; it is also that they don't see anyone else who can do the work. There is simply no one else.

The experience that this story wants to convey is this: God does not demand of anyone that they bear the entire responsibility and be overwhelmed by it. Rather, God wants the responsibility distributed on many shoulders. God opens our eyes to the fact that there are in the church persons who are not simply helpers but who are able to assume true collegial responsibility – even when it does not seem possible. When one begins to realize that he or she cannot do it alone, and he or she does not need to do it alone, then that is the moment that the Holy Spirit is there. To be charged with the leadership of the church means counting on the gifts of the Spirit, on persons in the church who can help, who understand themselves to be equally responsible.

## III.

God's Spirit stirs up the church again. It breaks in in desperate situations. It brings to an end the one-man system. And, it inspires fresh awakenings. Moses chooses seventy persons who are prepared to assist him. The fact is he is not alone. Indeed, they do not come to him. He must go to them, speak with them, call them together and tell them that God has plans for them. He does not enlist them; rather, they are to be ready for what God has in mind for them: "Gather for me seventy of the elders of Israel...and bring them to the tent of meeting, and have them take their place there with you...and I will take some of the spirit that is on you and put it on them; and they shall bear the burden of the people along with you so that you will not bear it all by yourself."

They must gather in the presence of God. Nothing happens unless they come together. They are then given a portion of the same spirit Moses received from God. With that, Moses does not become poorer, but richer. He does not now retain only one-seventieth of the gift of the Spirit that he had, but rather there are seventy others who receive a portion of the Spirit that God bestows. And God's Spirit does not quench individuality, the peculiar nature of each person, but rather elevates it and makes it useful for the whole. God instructs the seventy-one to work together and enables them to do so. They need each other and they enrich each other; they limit each other and they complete each other with the gift of the Spirit bestowed by God.

We are told that upon receiving the Spirit these men become ecstatic as prophets. They did not become immediately active Nor did they start their activities at once. God's Spirit inspired them with enthusiasm. Presumably, that expressed itself in a way that would be strange to us today. "They are filled with new wine," said the people at Pentecost when they saw the apostles filled with the Holy Spirit (Acts 2:13). They were beside themselves. Good to know that God's Spirit not only blows where it wills, but also how it wills, that it does not depend on our average norms, that it does not conform to a north European average Christian. God's Spirit can also express itself in ways that are to us unusual and peculiar. It cannot be domesticated and normalized.

By no means must the Spirit always or predominantly be expressed in extraordinary ways. That it causes people to become ecstatic simply means, first of all, that they leave their comfort zones; they break out of their self-contained framework; God opens for them new areas in which to maneuver; they receive possibilities for entirely new experiences. They are already a bit beside themselves, no longer caught up in themselves. It is the gift of a new service; a fresh, intensive ability to listen to God; a fresh ability to read attentively; an ability to pray in a way that goes beyond the boundaries of our heretofore linguistic ability; a new refined ability to perceive God and God's activity in the world; an unheard of sensitivity to what God now wants the church to do; a new and fresh support for those who are neglected and who suffer in the world, the capacity for an effusive joy in God that breaks down all barriers

To be sure, I ask myself, Exactly how was the ecstasy that was caused by God's Spirit, the ecstatic boundary-breaking of these seventy men, supposed to help Moses not have to bear responsibility for the people of God all by himself? Would not the "spirit of power, of love, and of self-discipline" (II Tim. 1:7) have been more needful? For the leadership of the community would not soberness be needed more than ecstasy? God's Spirit provides both: the calmness of the directors and the enthusiasm of the singers, the essential planning and the spontaneous idea, the analyst and the dreamer. The church needs both. But when she finds herself dragging on arduously when no one wants to lead anymore, when resignation sets the tone, then obviously the greatest help is the Spirit of Pentecost which gives wings to, sweeps along, inspires people – from within and beyond – and transforms them into a choir of the new creation. What's needed is not people with a cool head, but with warm hearts, not those advised by the past, but those who look to the future and are seized by it and are thus roused for the challenges of the present. Not guardians of the institution, but recipients of inspiration, not people who depend on what is calculable, but those who wait for the surprising, the promised one.

God's Spirit stirs up the church again. Over and over she comes to a standstill, as then. There's no more going forward. And then God distributes God's Spirit. At that time it fell to seventy men. I believe that today there are more. We need only watch, and then we never cease to be astonished: young people give up their vacation to work with disabled children; a mother tells her son about Jesus; some sing every Sunday in worship; some in a community pray day and night without a break during the decade of peace; some renovate their church; a couple of parents write to the government to propose leading a course in "education for peace" instead of the military instruction; some go into the streets to invite people to a gospel meeting. A choir of trombones plays hymns to a man on his 80th birthday; some are planting trees here; over there others are gathering sewing machines for partner churches in Tanzania. Someone is comforting a young mother at the grave of her child with the Word of God. Someone else is painting images of the stations of the cross for his church.

I could go on and on about all that is happening in our church through God's Pentecostal Spirit. There is much that is being stirred up. It is simply beautiful. "The Spirit and gifts are ours through him who with us sideth"[9] And God has much more in store for us.

And not only for us. The story concludes with two men who for whatever reason were not part of the tent meeting, but who had also been filled with God's Spirit, becoming ecstatic and experiencing boundless joy. Perhaps they danced and clapped their hands, or one took a guitar and the other drums, and they sang Hallelujah! and did not want to stop. Who knows? Joshua, obviously a firebrand for strict liturgical order, wanted to restrain this uncontrolled enthusiasm of the Spirit. He said, "Moses, my lord, stop them!" That is wrong! But Moses evidently realized that there was much less danger for the life of the community in spiritual exuberance than in spiritual coolness and well-tempered churchiness. He said, "Would that all the Lord's people were prophets, and that the Lord would put his spirit on them!" Therefore, do not be afraid of a bit of enthusiasm or what appears to be such. Instead, let us ask God to pour that Spirit on all of us: the spirit of self-discipline and the spirit of boundless joy. Amen.

---

[9]Translator's note: From Luther's hymn "A Mighty Fortress Is Our God".

# Isaiah 43:1
## April 26, 1987
### First Sunday after Easter at the City Church in Wittenberg

But now thus says the Lord, he who created you, O Jacob, he who formed you, O Israel: Do not fear, for I have redeemed you; I have called you by name, you are mine.

Dear Friends! It is good that at this worship service on the first Sunday after Easter those especially invited here are those who were baptized here in the past year or who as parents and godparents participated in a baptism. They can be reminded with us and we with them of our own baptism, of that which happened with us and to us. Perhaps there are some among us who not been baptized. For them this service could be an invitation to enter into what life holds for them. Naturally, it is fortunate that a small girl has been baptized here today, so that we could see how God begins a life story with a person. The parents of this child have chosen as a baptismal verse the word that is written in the book of the prophet Isaiah: Do not be afraid, for I have redeemed you; I have called you by name; you are mine!

Even when this word is addressed to the people of God who did not know about baptism, we can still detect something of a brief summary of the meaning of baptism.

God says to God's people: "You are mine." I think it's important to note that God says this to **his** people, to his community, not to any Tom, Dick, and Harry. In baptism God establishes a personal, but not private relationship with us. "You are mine" is aimed at a particular individual, but a particular individual in the people of God, in the church of Jesus Christ. Baptism is not for the lone wolf who wants to be able to live his private Christianity for himself or herself – apart from the community –, but rather it incorporates one as a member of the people of God. That we belong to God can only be experienced in community, and nowhere else. Thus, baptism belongs in the worship of the community. "You are mine." As a member of the community you are mine. You now belong to my people, God says to us in baptism.

Then we must also note that it is God who speaks here: **I** have redeemed you; **I** have called you by name, you are **mine**. In baptism the initiative comes from God. God is at the beginning. In baptism we do not seal our decision for God; rather, God seals God's decision for us: "You are mine." We do not stretch our hand out to God; rather, God lays God's hand on us. God always goes ahead of us and anticipates us – a courteous God. It cannot be described any better than Paul Gerhardt has in his Christmas hymn: "When I had not yet been born, you were born in me, and claimed me for yourself before I knew you. Before I was created by your hand, you had already considered how you wanted to be mine."[10]

Because this is so – because God had us in mind before we were created, because God says to us "my child" before we are able to say "Our Father", that is why we justifiably baptize little children such as this one today. "You are mine," God claims, even when they cannot yet understand. Naturally, he hopes they will one day respond, "I am yours." But that is not a prerequisite. It is a radiant Yes that God says to us in our baptism – without preconditions or works. This radiant, unconditional Yes that God says to us in baptism is, of course, something of a risk for God. All those baptized persons who live as if that has never been said to them speak a very sad language.

But God accepts this risk. "You are mine," God says to each person who comes or is brought to baptism. You belong to me – you no longer belong to yourself; you don't belong to any other, not even to the state or the nation. And for parents who bring their child to be baptized, you may not treat this child as your possession, but rather as a gift that has been entrusted to your loving care. "You are mine," you belong to me – not like a refrigerator or a car. You do not belong to me as a lifeless object, but rather as the living, particular, unique person that you are.

---

[10] Translator's note: this is my translation. The German here is the second verse of the hymn "Ich steh an deiner Krippen hier".

"I have called you by name." For me you are not a number, not just anyone. With me you have a name, not simply a personal identification number. God know us. God knows what life looks like for us, what lies deep within our hearts. But God also knows what we need to make something good out of our lives. That is why God establishes in our baptism a personal relationship with us: "I am yours, you are mine." A relationship in life that is spirited and energetic. "You are mine" – my child, my son, my daughter. You are entitled to my legacy. With me you are at home, in the midst of an inhospitable world. You are in the safe place of my love. You live near to my heart. "You are mine – forever and ever. I will no longer be God without you, and you will no longer be a human being without me. Never more without me. Not even in the deepest pain of your life. Not even in death. You are and will always remain mine. From my point-of-view that will never change.

That we belong to God and are in a living relationship with God has its basis in an actual activity of God: "I have redeemed you," God says to his people and to us as members of his people. I have seized the powers from the hands that grip and govern you, enslave and want to destroy you from the first days of your life – the pernicious powers of death and of evil. This act of liberation took place in the death and resurrection of Jesus Christ. What occurred there **for** us is what takes place **in** us in baptism. Thus, Martin Luther is able to say about baptism in his Small Catechism: "It works forgiveness of sins, delivers from death and the devil"; he says the same thing in the second article on Jesus Christ: "who has redeemed me, a lost and condemned creature, secured and delivered me from all sins, from death, and from the power of the devil."[11]

In baptism the event of liberation of Good Friday and Easter becomes an event in our own life. We are no longer at the mercy of hostile powers. No longer can they govern us and drive us to misfortune. "I have redeemed you," I have liberated you for freedom, God says through Jesus Christ, the crucified one who is risen from the dead.

---

[11]Translator's note: "Of Baptism" and "Second Article – of Redemption" in Luther's Small Catechism.

With our baptism our life is connected to him. Through our baptism we have a common story with him – a life story in the midst of and beyond a world filled with death. It is the story of a journey that he travels with us, gives us direction, lifts us up when we fall, comes after us when we are lost, and brings us to the goal of full freedom and complete joy in communion with him.

"You are mine" – it is not possible to comprehend in an entire human life everything that that entails. That that statement is true boggles the mind. No, it cannot be grasped. But it is true.

In our baptism God has in Christ impressed – and imprinted – his mark of ownership on us, "the indelible seal." It cannot be removed. In all circumstances we are marked with this sign of being a child of God – even when we have forgotten or disavowed our baptism and gone our own way, far from home, away from the community of faith. That we remain imperishably marked with this sign is our great chance – the chance of the prodigal son about whom Jesus tells in a parable: Even when he had turned his back on his father and lived a life without him, the father never stopped seeing him as his son and waiting for him to return home. And then when the son did return from his reckless life, the father embraced him and said, "This my son was dead" – dead in the midst of self-gratification and flourishing vitality – "and is now alive." "This my son." Even when he wanted to have nothing to do with his father, in the eyes and heart of the father he was still his son. That had not changed: you are mine.

Dear friends, I don't know how since your baptism your journey may have gone, whether your baptism has played or is playing a role in your life. I only know that each person can start over where God started with you, when God made you God's own and said, "You are mine." Each one of us may answer, and in this worship service we are invited to answer, "Yes, I am yours." I no longer want to belong to myself, to be my own master, to be driven by my ambition, my greed, my worry. I want to belong to you, to be entrusted to you, to listen to you, and to thank you for my life. Martin Luther called this the Reditus ad baptismum, the return to baptism, the renewal of the baptismal covenant, the putting into practice of the received baptism, the seizing of that which has been shared with us in baptism. Yes, I am yours! Here you have me!

Completely. Forever. In spite of all bad experiences in which you accompany me.

Whoever hears God's promise, "You are mine" and answers, "I am yours," whoever is true to their baptism or has renewed that vow, also lives with the words, "Be not afraid!" Those of you who were baptized 70 years ago or more and who know something of the fear of isolation and sickbed before death, Be not afraid! The one who said to you in your baptism, "You are mine," has also said, "even to your old age I am he, even when you turn gray I will carry you" (Isaiah 46:4).

You who have brought your tiny child for baptism and are concerned what will become of this child, what influences she will encounter, everything that could happen to her: Be not afraid! The one who said to this child in baptism, "You are mine," has also said, "No one will snatch them out of my hand" (John 10:28).

The Heidelberg Catechism opens with the question, "What is your only comfort in life and in death?" The answer is, "That I am not my own, but belong – body and soul, in life and in death – to my faithful Savior, Jesus Christ." Even when that is written in a Reformed confession, without blinking an eye Martin Luther said, "That is absolutely true." Amen.

# Isaiah 66:13a
## December 31, 1988
### New Year's Eve at the Cathedral at Magdeburg

As a mother comforts her child, so I will comfort you.

Dear friends, in looking back on the end of this year I cannot help but be moved by the images of recent weeks. If we were to see in a compressed summary once again everything that we have witnessed this year on television of the shocking course of events, we would hardly be able to stand it.[12]

With the suffering that is so vividly publicized we may easily forget that there is suffering among individuals in a very personal way and that there is more of it than what is reported in the media or brought to our attention. I suspect that in this worship service there are probably very few who would have to think very long whether and when they suffered in the past year, experienced pain, received horrific news, whether and when they have wept.

Surely most, if not all of us have had good and beautiful experiences this year. I have also. Tonight my wife and I will spend time reflecting together once again, and we will again rejoice and give thanks to God for everything. With the good experiences of this year I am quite satisfied. But there are other matters about which I am not so easily pleased, if at all. I have caused pain in my own life. I had planned so much that should have turned out differently, and yet nothing has changed me at all. But if things looked different to me – I do not mean for myself alone, but in a

---

[12] Translator's note: No doubt, one of the events Krusche had in mind was the downing of the Pan Am passenger plane over Lockerbie, Scotland on December 21. Also, he may have had been thinking of the weekly prayer services throughout East Germany calling for more openness on the part of the government. Other events of that year include the beginning of the collapse of the Soviet Union, violence in Northern Ireland, war between Eritrea and Ethiopia, the demise of Augusto Pinochet's oppressive rule in Chile when he loses a plebiscite, the shooting down of an Iranian passenger jet on July 3, an air show disaster at Germany's Ramstein Air Base when three jets collide.

network of relationships to other persons in the church and outside the church – their suffering concerns me and perplexes me.

This year I accompanied the coffin of a student – often he was in our home, a blossoming, gifted young man, the absolute joy of his parents. And then he had a fatal accident. I can only imagine what his parents must have felt this Christmas. With that I am not so pleased. I have experienced from a distance the break-up of a pastor's marriage. Two persons whom I liked very much and whose friendship I treasured. And now they have gone their separate ways. That makes me very sad.

I know how bleak things seem in many churches. This year I have seen how the church has begun to be treated, and I had believed that a bit of trust had emerged and that one could depend on certain declarations. I can hardly cope with what young people have told me about the treatment they have experienced from security officials – "otherwise we will be like Chile",[13] which was intended as a threat. I am also alarmed at how on all sides old hostile images are polished up in order to thwart the decreasing preparation for military service.

I will stop – it could otherwise seem that I put on dark glasses as I looked over this past year. No, I have not become a pessimist. Of course, mention could be made of good experiences, of joyful events, of signs pointing to hope. I have not overlooked those. But, as I have said, I am pleased and satisfied with those. When there is a problem here, it is namely this, that I not let the good experiences be hidden by the others, so that I no longer see them and forget to thank God for them. But the others are still there, and I cannot get rid of them at midnight with a glass of champagne. They travel with me into the new year. And I would very much like to enter the new year with good cheer.

And then I am confronted with the word from the prophet Isaiah in which God says, "As a mother comforts her child, so I will comfort you."

---

[13] Translator's note: The reference here is uncertain, but it may refer to the torture many in the church (and elsewhere) suffered in the regime of Augusto Pinochet in Chile. The phrase appears in a "Protest Declaration, dated October 29, 1988, by the "DDR-Weite Vollversammlung der Kirche von Unten" (the "GDR-wide Assembly of the Church from Below").

For me, this voice is among the most beautiful in all of the Old Testament. Ever since I became familiar with Brahms' **Requiem**, this verse has sunk deep into my soul. And, in all likelihood, not only into mine. It is intended for those persons who suffer as the people of God and with the people of God, for those who only with difficulty are satisfied with what they, personally and with others, experience as painful reality.

It is the first place in the Old Testament in which God identifies God's self as a motherly God. Otherwise, God addresses God's self or is spoken of in images of husband, father, landlord, king, warrior. (This certainly had sound reason – probably, in order to make clear that the God of Isaac, the true God, did not want to have anything to do with abundant fertility religiosity and its female deities.) I cannot identify with it (as I am not a woman), but Kurt Lüthi of Switzerland obviously knows what it's like, although he is not a woman either: "Self-conscious women," he writes, "cannot identify any more with a God described in male terms." Frankly speaking, as a man I cannot identify with this God either. I don't know when we had to identify ourselves with God. God has identified with us in the person of Jesus. I think it childish to ask whether God could not also have become human as a woman – as a Jesa Christa –, but I am happy that God describes God's self in motherly terms.

As a man, I am fortunate to have a God that comes to his people in their pain not with appeals, summons, commands – "don't whine," "get yourself together," "stop with your infernal howling," not one who declares he doesn't want to hear any laments, but rather songs of praise. How good it is that we have a God who comforts not as a man, but as a mother. We have a motherly God – even if we do not pray "Our Mother who art in heaven" – and in Jesus we have a motherly figure – "Jerusalem, how often have I desired to gather your children together as a hen gathers her brood under her wings" (Mt. 23:37). Anselm of Canterbury also has a beautiful saying (I have it from my wife who found it somewhere):

And you, Jesus, beloved Lord,

are you not also a mother?

Truly, you are a mother;

the mother of all mothers,

who underwent death,

to give their children life.[14]

Clearly, God has observed mothers well as God compares them to himself. "As a mother comforts her child, so I will comfort you." How does a mother comfort? She draws her child into her heart, she shares its pain and feels it, and at the same time she lets the child know the warmth of her motherly love. She lets the child have a good cry. She lets the child express from the heart all its concerns. It is never too much for the mother. She listens with a gentle voice.

A mother has many ways of offering comfort. She never simply says, "O you poor child, you are so much trouble." Offering comfort is so much more than showing sympathy and having compassion and uttering "comforting words" for which pastors (and now also secular speakers make in black-bordered announcements) are thanked and understood at the moment as sincere, but which do not change the situation. No, whoever knows a mother's compassion sees the world differently. Life goes on. Comfort is help in continuing with life. The comfort happens differently each time, depending on who is to be consoled and why: whether it's a small child who has fallen down and scraped a knee, or a disabled eight year old boy who is ridiculed in school and knocked down, or the 17-year old daughter whose boyfriend has broken up with her and has deeply wounded her feelings, or the married couple whose beloved young daughter has died. Mothers know how to comfort them and what must happen to make the situation bearable.

The mother-like God is so abundant and takes such a variety of forms that no one among God's people is left alone to suffer and die, but rather they regain their way again and continue with hope and courage.

---

[14] Translator's note: A very similar, though not exactly the same, prayer is found in Anselm's "Prayer to St. Paul: Our Greatest Mother". The above is my translation.

There are parents who must watch with profound grief as one of their children takes a path that leads farther and farther away from God and the church. This year they saw their son/daughter leave the church. They reproach themselves and ask whether out of extreme caution they wanted to protect their children or put too much pressure on them. The parents missed something crucial. And then at some point they come across – in their own reading of the Bible or in worship or some other way – the parable of the man who has a hundred sheep and leaves the ninety-nine to search for the one who has wandered off from the flock, getting lost. The shepherd never stops looking for the lost sheep until he finds it and returns it to the flock. Of course, they were already familiar with this parable, but now they saw what the mother-like, compassionate God wanted to say to them through it: I have never stopped loving your son/daughter. He/she has remained my child. I continue to search for them, I will not leave them in their lostness. Love them as you always have. Pray for them, but do not rebuke or pressure them. What they need now is anticipation of mother-like acceptance, not father-like coaching.

There's a woman who became very lonely. In the past year she celebrated Christmas with her husband, but now she lives alone in her home. No one is there to say "Good morning" and "Good night." One Christmas Eve she was with her children and grandchildren. While that was nice, they could not replace the most trusted person in her life. On the day after Christmas she took down the photo album and with every picture she was reminded of the way things once were. What a beautiful life she and her husband had! God's mother-like comfort was evident in that all of that became clear and she began to give thanks for everything that had made her life rich and deep. Comfort. Memories lead to gratitude.

A 17-year old girl. There is no longer any doubt – she is pregnant. Her friend pressures her to go to a clinic, but she doesn't want to. She finally goes to her mother. Her heart is in her throat. Her mother's first reaction is not "A fine mess this is," but rather, "I am delighted about your baby." "With a mother's hands he faithfully leads his own to and fro" one sings as his experience in one of our hymnals.[15]

Perhaps there is someone here who has done something this year that weighs heavily on your heart. Perhaps you have deeply wounded someone or betrayed their trust or seriously wronged them. The harm that has been done cannot be undone. The mother-like, consoling God leads them to a person whom they immediately trust and to whom they can confess the unvarnished truth, a person who not only has life experience, but also has cross experience. And with this person they will experience what we sang in Jochen Klepper's New Year hymn: "Whatever we neglect, whatever we miss, need no longer oppress you"[16] – the Crucified one has taken it on himself and forever removed it from the world. I do not know how I could have survived this year without this comfort.

And what worries us as we look at our church to which we belong and which means something to us – the shortage of spiritual strength, so little life that is authentic, the indifference of so many of its members, the disparaging treatment which it again experienced this past year – that should not leave us despondent: "Can and would a mother ever desert her child and even reject it, that it could no longer find grace? And if it were to happen that she fell away, God swears by his life that he will not let you go. Therefore, do not be afraid, O you Christian flock! God will provide aid and protect you."[17] It is only bleak if we no longer trust God – no resurrection, no renewal, no undergirding.

There is, of course, a depth of suffering which no consolation can penetrate. "My soul refuses to be comforted" (Ps. 77:2c). And according to the account of the massacre of the children in Bethlehem, the evangelist (Mt. 2:18) recalls the words of the prophet Jeremiah: "A voice is heard in Ramah, lamentation and bitter weeping. Rachel is weeping for her children; she refuses to be

---

[15] Translator's note: This is my translation. It is part of stanza 5 of Johann Jacob Schütz' hymn "Sei Lob und Ehr dem höchsten Gut". Although the hymn is in the Evangelical Lutheran hymnal, this stanza is not included.

[16] Translator's note: The translation is mine. The stanza is found in verse 5 of Klepper's hymn "Der du die Zeit in Händen hast".

[17] Translator's note: This is stanza 3 in the German hymn "Lob Gott getrost mit Singen. The translation is mine.

comforted..." (Jer. 31:15). The mother-like God endures our suffering with us and takes our suffering to heart. Through Jeremiah God says, "Therefore I am deeply moved for him; I will surely have mercy on him, says the Lord" (Jer. 31:20c). There is a depth of suffering that can only be borne under the promise: "God will wipe every tear from their eyes. Death will be no more; mourning and crying and pain will be no more; for the first things have passed away" (Rev. 21:4). "Blessed are those who mourn, for they will be comforted" (Mt. 5:4). Comfort through the promise of the final obliteration of suffering.

For the most part our suffering will not have such unfathomable depth. God's mother-like comfort can then appear such that God shows us the suffering of others and we can see how small our own suffering is in comparison to others. Comfort through becoming aware of the pain of others. And perhaps God pushes us further to visit the one who is hurting, so that we can experience where that person's strength comes from. Comfort from the example of another. And occasionally God comforts us simply so that God gives us a task which demands all our powers and thus allows us to forget about ourselves. How many have been consoled in this way, that God expects them to be there for another person. "Encourage the fainthearted, help the weak," the church in Thessalonica is urged (I Thess. 5:14).

Comfort that is received converts into support, encouragement, help for life.

God knows – as a mother knows – what comfort we need by looking at what has weighed heavy on our hearts in the past year, and by looking at the new year with its worrisome possibilities. In a moment we will pray Paul Gerhardt's hymn for a new year in which mention is made of God's mother-like comfort:

For as from faithful mothers

in heavy thunderstorms

protect their little child

with loving care,

no less does God let his children

sit in his bosom

when danger and sadness strike.[18]

Dear brothers and sisters, Hidden in God's heart, peacefully in God's hand, we may continue our journey with each other from year to year. Amen.

---

[18] Translator's note: This is stanza 4 of the hymn "Nun lasst uns gehn and treten mit Singen". It is my translation.

# Jeremiah 23:5-8
## November 30, 1986
1st Sunday in Advent at the Protestant Church
at Saxau in Breisgau[19]

The days are surely coming, says the Lord, when I will raise up for David a righteous Branch, and he shall reign as king and deal wisely, and shall execute justice and righteousness in the land. In his days Judah will be saved and Israel will live in safety. And this is the name by which he will be called: "The Lord is our righteousness."

Therefore, the days are surely coming, says the Lord, when it shall no longer be said, "As the Lord lives who brought the people of Israel up out of the land of Egypt," but "As the Lord lives who brought out and led the offspring of the house of Israel out of the land of the north and out of all the lands where he had driven them." Then they shall live in their own land.

Dear Friends, This word from the prophet Jeremiah comes to us from a distance of more than 2500 years. It would have been spoken around year 595 BCE. Those who heard it for the first time – the first ones – certainly heard it quite differently than we hear it. The word that God proclaims through his prophets is always a word that goes out into history and, at the same time, makes history. Between the audience of that time and today's audience lies the history of Jesus Christ, from which this word has been taken up, in which it has been kept, and by which it has been interpreted. It preceded the story of Jesus Christ, entered into it and accompanied it, and therefore did not disappear. And so it now comes to us. It can no longer be detached from this story which has become our story – not the story after Christ, but the story with Christ and up to him.

---

[19] Translator's note: Breisgau is near Freiburg in southwest Germany, which at the time was in West Germany.

Jeremiah told this promise of a branch coming from David when among the people of God a paralyzing hopelessness had begun to spread. The successors to the throne of David had completely gone downhill. The last of them, during whose reign Jeremiah spoke this word, was a weak-minded tool of his officers and civil servants. Everything looked very bleak. To be sure, there were political prophets who painted everything rosy or bright blue. But everyone knew that this was not the reality as they experienced it. Their experiences devoured all hope. Jeremiah did not see his task as being to blend into the gray a few dark colors and to paint a black picture nor to paint a pretty picture or sketch some ideal image. Instead, he announced: Things will not remain as they are. Not because he had discovered somewhere on the political horizon a silver lining, a glimmer of hope, but rather because God has said, "The days are surely coming when I will raise up for David a righteous Branch, and he shall reign as king," and not as those they had experienced up to now. And the work of his rule will be justice and righteousness. No longer will the ruler be one who governs with capriciousness, recklessness, or abuse of power, but rather the coming king will work for justice for all of them as persons living in peace with each other. Noteworthy in this promise is the absence of any reference to military strength or war-like success of this king – no mention of overcoming enemies and subjugating nations. The peace that he brings will be final.

The hope that things will not remain as they are comes not from history, from some ray of light, but from God's promise which is fully realized in history – not above it and not beyond it. It is a hope that is grounded in and related to history, a hope that emerges from the promise: a successor to David, as king of righteousness, will change and end the hopeless story.

The promises that God expresses through the prophet Jeremiah made Israel in the midst of nations into a waiting people, one in whom again and again hope overcame paralyzing experiences and turned their attention to the future. This hope prevailed for centuries after Jeremiah's prophecy. During that time the people of God became a toy among the powers without its own king. That hope entered the gas chambers in the hell of Auschwitz and was not burned.

The hope for a king who would establish justice and righteousness, quickened by the prophetic word, led the ancient people of God to gauge each of their leaders against this image and to ask, Are you the one? And none fit it. Then when the time came that the promise was fulfilled, they did not recognize him. For God made real the promise in a way that was very different from what they had expected – and also quite different from what Jeremiah himself could have understood when he prophesied. They had expected a political ruler who would re-establish the external relationships.

Then Jesus came, a descendant of David, to be sure, but a king? One who traveled the dusty roads – by foot. One who had nowhere to lay his head. One whose followers were a small band of powerless persons. And one could certainly not say that he established justice and righteousness in the land – in the end, he himself became the victim of a justice that dealt with false witnesses. Understandable is the question of John the Baptist whom the ruling king had thrown into prison because he had reproached him for his injustice: "Are you he who is to come" who will establish justice and righteousness, – "or shall we wait for another?" "Blessed is anyone who takes no offense at me," Jesus tells him. Blessed is the one who is not confused by the fact that God fulfills his promise so differently that he sets the hope of his people in a different kind of justice. Indeed, the one who was born in Bethlehem as the son of David is the one in whom the promise is fulfilled and is corrected. He is the one who is to come. There is no other to come. He is the only one. Whoever waits now for another waits in vain.

Whoever is gripped by his story knows this for certain: We come from him and we go back to him. The one who has come is coming. **We live in his Advent**, and in light of Jeremiah's prophecy we may reflect on the following:

1. How he establishes the new righteousness.

2. How he helps the weak realize their justice.

3. How he brings God's people together.

## I.

We are living in the Advent of Jesus Christ and see it as **he establishes the new righteousness**.

"The Lord is our righteousness" is to be the programmatic name of the one announced by Jeremiah. If he is our righteousness, then our own self-righteousness in which we are entangled and with which we destroy the first and most beautiful human right comes to an end, so that we are able to live our life in the community with God – as God's children. Self-righteous persons do not need God, especially to confirm their condition of righteousness. They are convinced that they can be responsible for their own life, and that the predominantly good that they have done is proof of their righteous life. In addition, they need someone against whom they can measure themselves and in comparison with whom their assessment is confirmed: it's just fine the way you are living. Each of us, no doubt, already has in mind a few such persons against whom we can compare ourselves. We all know how this self-righteousness and comparison with others can destroy community. Therefore, the one whose name is "God is our righteousness" tells the story of the Pharisee and the tax collector and, with it, proclaimed the new righteousness: righteous is the one who places God above self and appeals to the justice of God: "God, be merciful to me, a sinner." Whenever we realize that we no longer have a claim before God and lay our claim to the justice of grace, whenever we hold on to the one whose name is "God is our righteousness", we have experienced salvation. We then receive the human right to live in community with God. There is joy in heaven – and not only in heaven!

With that, a new element enters the story: wherever human beings live out of the justice of grace and therefore no longer are responsible for their own justification and must confirm it for themselves, and wherever they no longer need others mercilessly as a dark foil, then community is possible. Human beings who no longer find it necessary constantly to defend themselves – out of this graceless compulsion – can live with each other. And the further one is "above", the greater are the effects. Human beings who live out of the right to grace are a blessing for life in a society.

## II.

We are living in the Advent of Jesus Christ and see it as he helps the weak realize their justice.

"He shall execute justice and righteousness in the land," Jeremiah said of the one who is to come. He will intercede for the right of a person to be a whole person. Again and again this right is denied the weak at any given time in all societies. Their right to be seen as full human beings lay on the heart of Jesus. Thus, he ate at the table of those whom society had shoved to the margins. That is why he came to the defense of the woman found guilty of moral degradation by her untruthful accusers. That is why he associated with lepers who were carefully isolated from society, made contact with them and labored to see that they were able to return as healed persons to the rest of the community. And that is why he tells the story of the Good Samaritan. His story has an unmistakable connection to those who are weak and in the lower strata of society.

With the coming of Jesus Christ something unforgettable enters our story, something that is unique to the story, namely, sensitivity to the suffering of the weak and for justice for them; the sensitive reaction of his followers when they see this justice violated. They have been infected with the fire of love for the weak. And this fire extended beyond the community. Since then, the dark history of humanity with its bias against the weak is no longer hopeless. Everywhere – and certainly in this community as well – there are individuals or groups that no longer put up with the cynical or bureaucratically correct contempt of persons, no longer willing to stand by as others are kicked, insulted, tormented, chased, mercilessly cast aside, thrown out onto the street, their human dignity wounded.

Infected by Jesus, the dumb can speak, the weak become defenders, the helpless become helpers, insurgents against injustice – with the resources by which the crucified King of righteousness can say Yes, and with prayers for the oppressed – prayers for their inner strength and that they remain protected from hatred and desire for revenge – and for their oppressors, that they become aware of how very much they are destroying their own human dignity. Our efforts cannot create a world-wide fellowship in which all human beings are friends with each other. However, there is much evidence that the one whom the prophet announced is at work, that he will exercise justice and righteousness in life. We will not establish world-wide fellowship, but he will – with his final Advent. With that, we may persevere.

III.

We are living in the Advent of Jesus Christ, and experience it **as he brings God's people together**.

"Therefore, the days are surely coming when it will be said, 'As the Lord lives who brought out and led the offspring of the house of Israel out of the land of the north and out of all the lands where he had driven them.'"

Presumably, these words were not spoken by Jeremiah, but by a later spokesperson who had passed on the prophetic word of the king of righteousness to a new situation: to the people of God who had been hopelessly deported to a foreign country. You belong to the God who will bring you home.

Here we can see very well how the prophetic word that was spoken at one time in a very definite historical situation does not remain there, but moves with the people of God in new situations. This promise was fulfilled when those deported returned to the land God had given their ancestors and from which they had been taken. But as the exodus of God's people from slavery in Egypt leads beyond that to an even greater realization, so too does this fulfillment lead beyond itself to a final gathering of the people of God who are scattered throughout the world.

Jesus took up the prophet's words and took them further: "Then people will come from east and west, from north and south, and will eat in the kingdom of God" (Lk 13:29).

Every time we celebrate the Lord's Supper it takes place in the anticipatory joy of the great festival of life in communion with God that will never end, in which persons from around the world will take part. And every ecumenical gathering, even in the smallest group, is full of hope; in it is proclaimed something of the unity of humankind in praise of God.

And with that the confession widens to the God who fulfills God's promise in history; no more: God who has freed God's people from slavery in Egypt, no more: the God who returned God's people from exile in Babylon, but rather: God who in Jesus Christ reconciled the world to himself. And finally: God – all in all.

We are pilgrims among God's people under God's promise through history – from fulfillment to fulfillment. On the way to the second and final Advent. Yes, we have a good life. Amen.

# Jeremiah 29:4-14a
## February 10, 1985
### 5th Sunday after Epiphany at the Kreuz Church in Dresden

Thus says the Lord of hosts, the God of Israel, to all the exiles whom I have sent from Jerusalem to Babylon: Build houses and live in them; plant gardens and eat what they produce. Take wives and have sons and daughters; take wives for your sons, and give your daughters in marriage, that they may bear sons and daughters; multiply there, and do not decrease. But seek the welfare of the city where I have sent you into exile, and pray to the Lord on its behalf, for in its welfare you will find your welfare. For thus says the Lord of hosts, the God of Israel: Do not let the prophets and the diviners who are among you deceive you, and do not listen to the dreams that they dream, for it is a lie that they are prophesying to you in my name; I did not send them, says the Lord.

For thus says the Lord: Only when Babylon's seventy years are completed will I visit you, and I will fulfill to you my promise and bring you back to this place. For surely I know the plans I have for you, says the Lord, plans for your welfare and not for harm, to give you a future with hope. Then when you call upon me and come and pray to me, I will hear you. When you search for me, you will find me; if you seek me with all your heart, I will let you find me, says the Lord.

Dear Friends! On January 16 in a worship service in the cathedral in Magdeburg Christians remembered the destruction of their city 40 years ago. On February 13 you will remember the destruction of this city in the Kreuz Church. With their rich history and beautiful buildings both cities were reduced to rubble and ashes in one night. Thousands of persons perished on this one horrific night. Here it's the rubble of the Frauenkirche, for us in Magdeburg it's the ruins of the Johanniskirche that remind us of the suffering endured and the guilt that accompanied it.

In the meantime 40 years have come and gone. With extraordinary effort the cities have been re-built. Much has become beautiful, and some even more beautiful than before. Those who knew the old Dresden or the old Magdeburg also clearly know what could not be restored. How do we live as God's church, as God's people, in our city in which it is not simply the external image of the city that has so drastically changed? Have we found our way in it, or have we simply put up with it? Have we become at home in it, or do we feel like strangers in it? And where do we as a church see our challenge in the city?

There is a remarkable parallel between Magdeburg and Dresden. In front of the ruins of your Frauenkirche and the ruins of our Johanniskirche stands a statue of Martin Luther. Luther stands with an open Bible in his hand, the book in which God's history with God's people and the world and the experiences of God's people with God in the world are told. If it is an accident that this statue of the man with the Bible stands in front of the ruins of these two churches in our cities, I would like to take this coincidence as an invitation to listen to the biblical word anew with all our questions and in our search for direction.

On this Sunday before February 13 in their worship services the churches in Dresden consider the letter of the prophet Jeremiah which I read a few moments ago. It is aimed at those among the people of God who had a severe political catastrophe behind them and an entirely uncertain future before them. Jeremiah had seen this catastrophe coming and had passionately intervened in an effort to prevent it. He had called on the politically responsible leaders for those not resisting to submit to the king of Babylon. But a man of God, still one with a pacifistic tendency, was in the eyes of the responsible leaders naturally incompetent to deal with political matters. What was necessary was a mind for reality and political expertise, and, of course, they possessed both. But it happened just as he announced it would. Now the entire leadership class together with the technical intelligence and the corresponding specialists and craftsmen were transported from Jerusalem to Babylon – resettled, we would say today.

They had been allocated land there, and now they were supposed to live in these strange, unfamiliar surroundings – as a religious minority in a country in which very different gods than the God of

Israel were worshiped. Despondent, powerless, embittered, they ask how God could have done this, how God could have put them, as the people of God, at the mercy of unbelievers. And, as always, when all seemed hopeless, they were also prone to political cliches which spoke in riddles of imminent upheavals. The superpower, Babylonia, would be so weakened by internal power struggles that the situation of the newly re-settled persons would not last long, and they would be able to return to their old, familiar circumstances. Perhaps they were also looking with some envy at other members of God's people who had been spared this difficult fate and who were able to live under more favorable conditions.

Today the community of God in Dresden and in Magdeburg is in a different situation than that of those who were deported to Babylon. History does not repeat itself. The letter of the prophet Jeremiah was written 2580 years ago, and it was addressed to Babylon and not to Dresden or Magdeburg. But what God had to say through his prophets to his people in a very particular historical situation is not so unique that it has nothing to say to later generations and would only be of historical interest to them; rather, what was said then has insights that for the attentive listener discloses an orientation and assistance in a wholly different historical situation.

I would now like to share with you what has become clear to me in reflecting on this prophetic word. The basic lesson for me is this: In whatever city we may live, God has goodness in mind.

God frees us in such a way that we

1. willingly accept our circumstances,

2. serve the common good responsibly,

3. bring before God our intercession for the city,

4. joyfully await God's future.

I.

Those people of God who were taken from their familiar surroundings and brought to a completely strange and therefore frightening place had to learn, first of all, that in their deportation they were dealing with God. It was not the evil conqueror nor a stab in the back by traitors in their own camp nor unreliable allies who were responsible for their miserable situation, but God. The prophet does not spare the deportees this hard truth, even if they were at the end of their rope, because there is a new beginning when this hard truth is acknowledged: God's justified judgment has come to us. We receive what our deeds deserve.

Twice we read, "Thus says the God of Israel to the exiles whom I have sent into exile from Jerusalem to Babylon...seek the welfare of the city where I have sent you into exile." The misfortune which you are experiencing comes from me. It is the misfortune that you intended for others or brought on others and has now fallen back on you. My judgment on you.

It was good for us that in his greeting to us in the Magdeburg cathedral a Dutch pastor recalled that a citizen of Magdeburg was the commander of the bomb squadron that destroyed his city of Rotterdam. Before Magdeburg and Dresden lay in rubble, Rotterdam and Coventry were destroyed by us. When we consider the destruction of our cities, we cannot judge the British and Americans, the allies at the time of the Soviet Union, but instead we must recall our own guilt. Not that we cannot grieve those who died at the time and were taken from us – why them and not us? One thing we may not do: accuse and dispute our guilt or explain it away by pointing to the guilt of others.

Certainly others have their own guilt, but that is their issue to deal with, and not ours to lay on them or to determine. The guilt of others is not our concern. Our issue is to acknowledge the guilt we Germans have and to confess it in an unvarnished way before God and humanity, and to admit everything that we feel about any injustice done to us as a consequence of our guilt. The forced removal, the expropriation, the treatment of prisoners of war and interred persons – so much injustice happened there, it is all related to our guilt.

Only when we no longer dispute this do we become free. When we know that it was not the despotism of the victorious powers, but God, that brought about the situation in which we find ourselves, then we are freed to accept it – to accept it willingly and not simply to put up with it reluctantly. God's judgments are always judgments of grace, they always contain the chance for new beginnings. In God's judgment the thought is not of suffering with us, but of peace. A community that understands itself to be under the judgment of grace does not want to return to the misguided past. It must no longer be indignant at the often burdensome present, and it does not escape to an imaginary future. It is freed by God to accept its situation with sober hope and courage in the face of what is temporary and fragmentary.

## II.

God has in mind what is good for us. God frees us to accept our situation willingly and thereby to serve the common good responsibly.

The exiles are challenged to build houses, plant gardens, and raise families. They should therefore settle down for the long haul. Their new situation will not simply be a brief Intermezzo. They should not listen to false prophets who, instead of speaking of God's judgment on the injustice of others, make the deportees contemptuous of the present and promise that they will soon return to their previous situation. What they are now experiencing is only an interim period of limited duration, not worth becoming engaged with it. Instead, they should wait it out and refrain from doing anything that would solidify relationships and contribute to a lengthening of their period of enslavement.

I think that we older folks know a little bit about such words. When I moved with my wife and child from Heidelberg to Dresden in 1954, along with a whole group of other pastor couples – the bishop called and everyone, everyone came – we were all, apparently of the same opinion that we would be there only a few years, on the announcement were words, "Germans at one table!" The reunification appeared imminent, and then the churches would surely return to their previous position. We simply needed to make it through the winter. Weather the intervening months, be patient, wait it out. Then life would resume. Then! And when winter lasted too long and the hoped for spring did not come, the watchword changed: Nothing is going to change. We cannot live here. What will become of our children? It makes no sense. We must get away from here! And many did. Even many Christians.[20]

But God's watchword was different: Stay here! Deliberately set up your homes here, so that you, your children, and their children will and can live in the GDR. Here I also have peace in mind for you. "Seek the welfare of the city!" In Hebrew the word is Shalom. Seek the Shalom of the city, its peace, its well-being. Thus, no more outer or inner emigration. Serve the common good! Do not put on airs or be bitter, but rather watch and see to it that life in your city and country are humane, that they proceed fairly, that here there is cultivated a climate such that all will want to stay and no one will want to leave. "Seek the welfare of the city!"

As members of God's community, wherever you can contribute to it in good conscience through your vocation, through participation in a common project, through your own initiative, through your personal conduct so that the person loved by God is able to come into his or her own, then do it! Even if there's no particular benefit to you, even if any kind of promotions are shut off to you, even if you say to yourself, "There's no point to this, nothing will ever change!" Do not let despair govern you! Simply do what is expected, what is necessary, what serves others, what promotes life together.

In the meantime I think we need no longer be afraid of the Marxists. If they plan and do something good, why would we not participate simply out of fear of losing our identity? Whoever seeks the welfare of the city naturally stabilizes the system, but they also

---

[20] Translator's note: Following World War II Germany was divided into four sectors, each being occupied by one of the victorious powers – Great Britain, the United States, France, and the Soviet Union. Soon it became clear that the part of Germany occupied by Great Britain, the United States, and France would become one unified region (West Germany), while the part of Germany occupied by the Soviet Union would become a separate region that was governed separately (East Germany). The city of Berlin was divided in the same way. Dresden, Leipzig, and Magdeburg, for example, were located in the East.

make it more dynamic. To seek the welfare of the city does not merely mean adapting, participating in everything, cheering everything, shutting off independent thinking. It also means being against and not participating in what harms the common good, in what is a burden to life together in the city, in what poisons the environment, in what infringes on the dignity of human beings.

Some time ago a pastor told me about a church elder who came to him and said, "I cannot take it anymore. I haven't slept well for a month. I am supposed to report whatever is said in the church council and whatever you innocently tell me. I cannot continue living this life of deception." Whenever a person is set against another to observe them and inform on them, something has irreparably harmed the human spirit and has profoundly destroyed every community.

To seek "the welfare of the city" means quite simply to reject all such demands. I say this to you in all seriousness. Whenever we see harm, wherever injustice or nonsense happens, we should help stop it and not wait until someone else stops it. I think I need not be more specific. Those who seek the welfare of the city are not those who either participate in everything or those who stay out of the way and say, "Let someone else...," but rather those who are prepared to share the responsibility and the work in critical solidarity, those who give their inner strength for what is best for the city. You, the Christians in this city, belong to them.

### III.

God intends good for us, frees us to serve the common good and to represent the city before him.

That we seek the welfare of the city, that we know that we share responsibility for its well-being is not peculiar to us Christians. We do this in solidarity with others. It is true for others and we should not deny that. Our activity is not to be differentiated from theirs, even if here and there each has its own unmistakable accents. But that which only we can do for the welfare of the city is on behalf of the city. "Seek the welfare of the city and pray to the Lord on its behalf." Here we are simply unique. If we fail to do that, no one else will do it, and that would not be good for the city. Prayer does not replace action, but it is in itself an activity that is not going to be done by anyone else. A city can expect that and it should know that God's community in the city prays for it. We owe that to it. The church is the mouth of the city to God. To pray for the city and the people who live and work there, to take particular responsibility for it and to suffer with it – to bring everything before God. There is no one who does not stand in need of it. We ask God's goodness for those with whom we want to live together in peace, whom we cannot look at as our enemies, even if they, incidentally, make life difficult for us. Our prayers of intercession change our relationship to them.

I believe that there is no one who can think so highly of the city as those who bring before God their citizens and their life together and the state of the city, its concerns and problems, think about before God and lay them before God's heart, who intercede for the city before God, appealing to God's fatherliness, begging for God's patience. Prayers of intercession provide strength and set the standard for our joint cooperation. Whatever we pray for must also be what we stand up for. Whatever we cannot pray for, we cannot also participate in.

But to pray for the Shalom of the city means more than praying for its well-being. Shalom not only means well-being, but also the healing of people and of the human community. Therefore, we will also pray that as much as possible many persons in this city and in this country come to a belief in Jesus Christ and receive from him life, the true life that keeps them and that no one and nothing, not even death, can take from them. Indeed, we pray to the God who loves the world and who wants to help all people and see that they live full, complete, fulfilled lives. To pray for the Shalom of the city also means to pray for an awakening.

## IV.

God has in mind what is good for us. God frees us to intercede on behalf of the city and to await with joy God's future. God not only encouraged those whom God led into exile in Babylon to see themselves under the judgment of grace and to accept the situation in this foreign city and to cooperate in its welfare. God not only warned them to steer clear of illusionary words of change anytime soon and of dismissing living in the present. Rather, God has given them a promise: It will soon become clear that God's judgment was really a judgment of grace, that God's plans for them were of peace and not of suffering. Their life in the foreign city will not be forever or without a future, but rather their future is the holy city, Jerusalem. After 70 years God will visit them and bring them home. Even if the recipients of this promise understood that they would not live to see it fulfilled, they also knew that it was not a vain promise. This promise did not move the present to some waiting room for the future. Instead, it formed a horizon of hope of active participation.

As a church of Jesus Christ in the earthly city, we do not have a promise of a turning-point in history, but certainly for the completion of history. Scripture calls it the heavenly Jerusalem, the new city, which we do not build, but which God prepares for us. The old city for whose Shalom we pray and work and which is, at best, a poor image of the eternal Shalom will not last forever. In hope for that eternal city we help build the old city, so that in it a bit of the Shalom of the future one is realized. With joyful anticipation we celebrate in the middle of the old city the meal of the present and coming Christ. Amen.

# Matthew 14:22-33

Sermon delivered at the Church Conference – Kirchentag[21] –
in Erfurt, 1983

Immediately he made the disciples get into the boat and go on ahead to the other side, while he dismissed the crowds. And after he had dismissed the crowds, he went up the mountain by himself to pray. When evening came, he was there alone, but by this time the boat, battered by the waves, was far from the land, for the wind was against them. And early in the morning he came walking toward them on the sea. But when the disciples saw him walking on the sea, they were terrified, saying, "It is a ghost!" And they cried out in fear. But immediately Jesus spoke to them and said, "Take heart, it is I; do not be afraid."

Peter answered him, "Lord, if it is you, command me to come to you on the water." He said, "Come." So Peter got out of the boat, started walking on the water, and came toward Jesus. But when he noticed the strong wind, he became frightened, and beginning to sink, he cried out, "Lord, save me!" Jesus immediately reached out his hand and caught him, saying to him, "You of little faith, why did you doubt?" When they got into the boat, the wind ceased. And those in the boat worshiped him, saying, "Truly you are the Son of God."

Dear Friends! If we consider this story, which Matthew the evangelist tells, under the heading "Dare to trust", we can make a few, and I think important, discoveries, discoveries which can then contribute to our own understanding. This much is clear: at issue here is not trust in general, but the trust of the disciples in their Lord. If we are to gain insights and grow in our understanding, it will most likely happen if we also dare to trust.

---

[21] Translator's note: Kirchentag is a multi-day Protestant church gathering every one to two years in Germany which began in 1949.

I.

Dare to trust means being prepared whenever the Lord presses us into public situations.

The disciples had imagined this evening to go quite differently than it did. They had witnessed something miraculous. Five thousand persons had come to Jesus. They had listened to him and many had been healed. And then he had miraculously fed them all. From very little which he had blessed and distributed to them they were full. What kind of Lord was that! We must picture it: the entire field still full of people laughing, happy with questions and astonishment. Just like a colorful, wonderful Kirchentag.

Jesus then sends his disciples away. Precisely now, in this moment. Here Matthew uses an unusually harsh expression: "On the spot," it reads literally, "he forced them into the ship." We can imagine it – how grudgingly they withdraw, how force is almost needed to get them into the boat. Whatever may have agitated Jesus to demand this dismissal at this exact moment – when everything was going so well – we do not know. In any case, the disciples were unable to make any sense of it. Why go to the other shore when there is life on this one? Away from terra firma where everything is secure to the lake where there are all kinds of dangers? And on top of that, at night, alone, and without him.

Daring to trust means being prepared, when the Lord commands us, to leave pleasant circumstances to which we had become accustomed and felt good about, and enter an entirely new situation with all its uncertainties (for example, a new social or vocational environment, in a hospital or a military post). Without knowing the meaning beforehand, even if it seems painfully absurd – it means trusting him that he very well knows what he is asking of us and why he is asking it of us right now. To trust that he has something in mind that will help us and provide us with new experiences with him. Of course, we know the end of this story and are in a better position than those first disciples.

## II.

Secondly, daring to trust means believing that Jesus never loses sight of us.

At other times, Jesus was always in the boat with them. This time he had let them go out into the night alone. That is the situation of the church after the ascension. There Jesus is no longer visible with them in the "ship that calls itself the church."[22] As long as nothing happens, as long as the lake is peaceful and calm, it may be fine simply to remember Jesus who is on the distant shore and for whom the historical distance grows greater and greater. That may be enough to remember the one who loved and helped people, who must have been a wonderful man. But when the storms come and stir up the lake and the breakers assail the boat and fear chokes the throat, such memories of the wonderful man Jesus don't help at all. There is still in the heart the crippling feeling of being defenselessly abandoned to sinister forces.

Thus, from this story we learn to believe that the Lord never lets the circle of disciples out of his sight. Matthew says, "And after he had dismissed the crowds, he went up the mountain by himself to pray. When evening came, he was there alone, but by this time the boat, battered by the waves, was far from the land, for the wind was against them." They are not alone. The Lord watches over them in their distress through the night – the rolling of the boat, his church. He prays for them. His intercession surrounds them in the midst of their chaotic confusion in which the hostile forces seize them. In John's Gospel we hear how he prays for his own: "Father, I am not asking you to take them out of the world, but I ask you to protect them from the evil one" (John 17:15). The Lord's intercession does not ask that the disciples sail peacefully on a wind-free fish pond, but rather that they not succumb to the forces breaking on the ocean of the world.

Daring to trust means believing that the Lord never loses sight of us, that when he seems far away, when there seems to be no trace of him, he is praying for us. Indeed, Jesus prays for us in the

---

[22] Translator's note: "Ein Schiff, das sich Gemeinde nennt" – a song by Martin Gotthard Schneider. My translation of the song title.

darkest of our nights and in the most difficult times of our lives. Of this we may rest assured: There is one who watches over us and prays for us.

## III.

Thirdly, daring to trust means persevering until the Lord comes to us.

The storm squalls raging on the lake and the furious masses of water continued to crash over the boat. The threatening situation persisted. The church, at the mercy of the powers, is tossed and driven to and fro. So it so often seems. And the Lord is not there. Our experience is that he is often inexplicably absent. Only in the fourth night watch did the Lord come, when the terrifying night was already three-fourths over.

The men in the boat may well have been inspired with their initial recovery from the storm that they survived such a violent experience and, so far, unscathed. But when the storm became increasingly worse, they struggled with dogged energy and exertion, doubting their ability to survive. The miraculous event they had witnessed with their Lord only a few hours before was long past, and they could not retrieve it. Experiences with Jesus Christ are simply not retrievable.

And so the men in the boat must continue to row, even if the boat doesn't seem to move. And then – in the fourth watch of the night, when they are so worn out that they could hardly row any more, the Lord comes. In the midst of hellish experiences, in hopeless situations when they are totally exhausted – all of a sudden a light. But they do not shout for joy, but rather they cry out, "A ghost!" It can only be a phantom that is haunting them, a mirage that is fooling them. When the church encounters danger, people only see ghosts. That the Lord could be coming to them does not seem possible. Only when they hear him speak do they recognize him "Take heart, it is I; do not be afraid!"

Daring to trust means persevering, keeping rowing, staying busy, even when it seems interminably long, when everything is going against us and we cannot take another step, when there is no silver lining on the horizon and we are at the end of our rope. Don't give up; instead, persevere in faith! "For you need endurance, so that you may receive what was promised," it says in the Letter to the Hebrews (10:36). The Lord will come, he will most definitely come, and he will most definitely not come too late. He will come over the abyss, the impassable, the unpaved. Nothing can stop him from coming to his own in distress. "You are the way of all ways" sings one who has experienced this,[23] and another, "Often we would lose courage in the face of fire and drowning, but you came to lead us out and fed us with heavenly food."[24]

We have often experienced that, when everything seemed to be over, when we could not continue and did not want to continue, but then suddenly he came to us with his word, and what had caused us so much anxiety was no more and our hearts could relax. At the time the disciples did not yet know that he would come. We, however, can with utmost certainty rely on the fact that he will come and that he never comes too late.

Even if for us it's a very long time. Because he will come, we will not perish.

## IV.

Fourthly, daring to trust means being certain that we find our footing with him.

"It is I; do not be afraid." Those words were directed at all who were in the boat. But one of them, Peter, took these words quite personally: Now I must go to him who has called to me. "Do not be afraid," he said. If it is the Lord, his word will bridge the abyss. "'Lord, if it is you, command me to come to you on the water.' And Jesus said, 'Come.' So Peter got out of the boat." A leaper, but a leaper of a particular kind. He does not get out because the boat will not hold him. Nor does he get out because he and the others in the boat are not getting along. Nor does he get out because he

---

[23] Translator's note: from the album "Befiehl du deine Wege" recorded by the North German Figural Choir. My translation.
[24] Translator's note: From stanza 5 of Matthias Jorisson's hymn "Jauchzt, alle Lande, Gott zu Ehren", based on Psalm 66. My translation.

wants to bring attention to himself through a particularly demonstrative act, by taking an extravagant step. Nor is it because he wants to provoke Jesus. He first asks him whether he may take this extraordinary leap of faith. A leaper in trust: If it is you, Lord, then keep your word and I will reach to you and find safety with you over the abyss, and I will not sink in the deep waters and I will find earth beneath my feet. Then I find a way that others cannot go. Then I can take steps that are truly impossible, steps that defy all rules and all experience.

The Lord does not consider criticizing Peter for being impertinent, for being one for whom it was obviously not enough to remain with the others in the boat, in the normal church, and experience the Lord's presence there. The Lord does not see getting out of the boat as being necessary for everyone, but he also expects from everyone more than the average and the ordinary and the normal. But he expressly approves when, in order to have an intensive proximity to him and to take seriously his words, "Be not afraid!", one reacts spontaneously and takes a daring step, thus trusting that the Lord will also make the abyss passable and guard his footing over the depths.

There is a little girl who leaves her studies and assists a disabled person in order to be near Jesus. There is a young woman who leaves a church situation in the Federal Republic (West Germany) and marries a pastor here because she has heard the Lord answer her question: Yes, take this step. There is a pastor who leaves his vocation because the congregation does not raise enough money to pay his salary for him to work: "Do not be afraid!" I will take care of you.

There is a student who out of general carefreeness climbs out of the boat and refuses military training in order to be near Jesus. There is someone who leaves the comfortable church life of his parents and says to Jesus, I am yours, I only want you, you alone, only you. And he leaves the soccer club because from now he goes to worship on Sundays.

These are real illustrations. Their decisions are not for everyone. Jesus does not call everyone to leap overboard. But they are legitimate examples of climbing out of the boat trusting the word of Jesus that sustains, that guards one's footing, and drives out fear.

## V.

Finally, daring to trust means crying out when we are sinking.

Whenever one takes an uncommon path, taking a risky step, things can go awry as they did with Peter. He left the boat trusting the word of the Lord. But then he heard the roaring of the storm and he saw the rolling of the waves and how precarious the ground is and how tremendous the depth beneath him was. And then his trust was no longer in the word that was supposed to support him and guard his footing. Whenever we take our eyes off Jesus and direct our attention to the menacing circumstances, we give in and lose our firm footing and begin to sink. Then there is no longer any stability.

Here daring to trust means crying out as Peter did: "Lord, help me!" And then there is the strong hand that grasps the one who is sinking. Whoever is sinking and cries out to Jesus, Jesus will not let them go under. However, that person is not spared the question, "Why did you doubt?" Why did you not truly trust me? Why did you so quickly let go of your faith?

But this question serves as an invitation to a new trust. The disciple who, thrilled by Jesus' voice, ventures to do the extraordinary but then breaks down, should know: He will not leave me in the lurch. Even when trust is not enough and I am devastated, I will not be confounded. Jesus' hand is there. That strong, good hand. It pulls me out of the undertow of the deep.

And no one in the boat celebrates when Peter returns to the boat. Rather, their hearts open up to each other as they see what kind of a Lord they have.

He deserves for us to trust him. Yes, he deserves that. Amen.

# Matthew 28:20; II Timothy 2:9
## May 31, 1984
Ascension of Christ in the Gemarker Church in Wuppertal-Barmen; a service in memory of the Theological Declaration of Barmen, 1934

And remember, I am with you always, to the end of the age. (Matthew 28:20)

The word of God is not chained. (II Timothy 2:9)

"The church's commission, upon which its freedom is founded, consists in delivering the message of the free grace of God to all people in Christ's stead and therefore in the ministry of his own Word and work through sermon and Sacrament.

"We reject the false doctrine, as though the church in human arrogance could place the Word and work of the Lord in the service of any arbitrarily chosen desires, purposes, and plans." (6th Thesis of the Barmen Declaration of May 31, 1934)

The sixth thesis of the Theological Declaration of Barmen begins with the statement of the risen Lord to his community of disciples, "Remember, I am with you always, to the end of the age" and with a word of the imprisoned apostle to his colleague, Timothy, "The word of God is not chained."

Friends, the Barmen Confession gave the church a breakthrough to freedom. Not the kind of freedom that offered the church all possibilities and privileges. In Barmen the church was given the kind of freedom that became oppressed, confined, and defamed, and was abandoned by the chokehold of power. She was given this freedom because she wanted to cleave wholly to the one who said, "So if the Son of man makes you free, you will be free indeed" (John 8:36). A church that wants to listen only to him is free of all forms of bondage. A church that binds itself to him is free, whatever its external circumstances may be. If a church depends only on Jesus and wants to hear only his voice, it will not become provincial or narrow-minded. It will then belong to him to whom all authority is given in heaven and on earth.

On this Ascension Day we are reminded that he is the Lord over everything – over all times, over all space, over all powers. Indeed, the sovereignty of the crucified one is not reflected in the image of clinched fists, but in the image of pierced hands. Sovereignty of free grace, sovereignty of that one who is guilty of nothing, but who takes on our guilt, all the guilt of unfulfilled love, and offers us unmerited and un-earnable life, life that stays with us, life that death can no longer take from us, life in community with him in grateful service to God's creatures in participation in his coming kingdom

This Lord's offer of life must go out to the people. And thus, to those who already belong to Jesus Christ, and to the church of forgiven sinners goes the charge to proclaim this message of free grace to all people: "Go and make disciples of all nations, baptize them..., teach them...."

Say to them, You are loved, you can let go of your guilt, freed to surrender, empowered to pray, invited to live with joy, engaged for the kingdom of God. And to the community of disciples who get on with this charge the Lord promises this: "I will be with you always, to the end of the age."

He says that to those who truly set out, who do not rest on the confession of their ancestors, but who themselves confess – "with heart and hands and voices"[25] – who he is and what he has prepared for everyone – "abundant life" (John 10:10).

"I will be with you," he says to them, and he says to us whenever you and I go to those who live on the edge, to the overlooked, the neglected, the cheated, to those who live a fragile and shattered existence, for those who have more than enough stability and self-righteousness and maybe a few disparaging remarks. I will be with you whenever you let their misery get under your skin and into

---

[25] Translator's note: from Martin Rinkart's hymn "Nun danket alle Gott" ("Now Thank We All Our God").

your heart and you promise them: "You are not forgotten. There is one who sees you and stays near you. He is not indifferent towards you. Open yourselves up to him. He wants to, and he can, help you in such a way that life is worthwhile. There is no reason to give up.

"I will be with you," he says, when you go to those in authority and must defend yourselves or call them to be responsible. My Spirit will be with you to give you the right words and to stand there unafraid and with unprovoked speech. I am with you when you go into prisons, clinics, homes where there is grief, and you comfort persons there and pray with them.

I am with you, the Lord says, when you go into the streets, in public, and testify to me as the Prince of peace who does not want us to be afraid of each other or to threaten each other with death, whose politics of peace always takes the first step. I am with you to comfort you when they call you "crazy" and say or write all kinds of evil things against you; my strength will be with you when you lose courage and you don't want to go on.

He is with us when we are with each other as the community of brothers and sisters, when we hear his Word, call on him, and receive him in Holy Communion. He is with us in the everyday world when we confess him in the places of ordinary life and are not ashamed of him. Always and everywhere we are in his field of vision, within hearing of his voice, in a secure place of his love, in the force field of his Spirit, in the light of hope of his future.

Because that is so, because he is with us in all places and at all times, God's word is not chained, but is the liberating word of his free grace.

It is not bound to any preconditions on our side. Very imperfect people, as we are, who stumble and stutter, who fail and sin, we are his messengers of this free word of grace. It's not because we are articulate or have an ability to persuade or because we are educated. My father was a simple country preacher, but with love and integrity he preached God's Word to me and to many persons in the Ore Mountains.[26] It is not chained to any bravery or fearlessness on our part. I know of people who at one time were

---

[26] Translator's note: the Erzgebirge, a region in the state of Saxony which is located in eastern Germany.

timid and then were able to say to their colleagues that Jesus was with them everywhere, even when they were shamed for it.

And this word is not bound to a particular age or life experience. I think of the child in her religious instruction class whom the teacher had called on to draw a picture of her loving God on the chalkboard. As she stood somewhat helplessly before the chalkboard, her teacher asked, "So, you cannot do it, can you?" to which the girl replied, "I need a golden chalk to do it."

God's word is not chained. Even for those who encounter it for the first time it is not dependent on their religious receptivity. To our own astonishment we see it over and over again as it enters the lives of young people who have otherwise had no contact with the church.

And the free word of grace is also not dependent on favorable external factors.

"The word of God is not chained," says the one who sits in prison.

With its comfort and wonderful promises it penetrated the lives of our brothers and sisters locked up in concentration camps. And from them it also reached other prisoners. I know no one in whom this word was so reflected as it was in Paul Schneider, the Reformed pastor from the Rhineland. He became known as the "preacher of Buchenwald." There was a man who tells this story about himself. He stood on the roll call square of the camp, all alone, at the end of his rope, firmly resolved to walk to the electric fence that night and bring to an end this wretched existence. Then over the square he heard a loud clear voice that over 20,000 others could also hear. It was Paul Schneider's voice. It called out from the window of his bunker cell, "Jesus Christ says, I am the light of the world. Whoever follows me will never walk in darkness but will have the light of life" (John 8:12).

The voice was then silenced by the blows of the bunker guard. The one who told that story added, "He saved me by his voice because from that point on I knew that he was with me."

No, the word of God is not chained. It does not depend on legally guarded freedom of speech. It's good when there is that, but it is neither the condition nor the guarantee for the freedom of God's word. The most liberal conditions do not protect the church from itself applying chains to God's word: to reduce it to the realm of the private, to exclude it from the arena of politics, to have it say only what does not cause trouble.

God's free word cannot exclude or confine.

It cannot fit one's own agenda. Neither can it be confined to whatever boundaries we wish to create. In its freedom it transcends national and confessional boundaries and narrow-mindedness, and makes possible common praise, common witness, common intercession for those separated from us, for those isolated from other people. The free word of God is not chained to our confessional bond, but rather makes us open to the Christian confession of others and leads us to new answers for new questions in new perilous times.

The church of the Barmen Declaration has good reason to thank God for this confession of the fathers and its guidance, good reason to confess to God that unfortunately too often we have not followed God, good reason to ask God that God help us in our day to confess Jesus Christ as the one in whom we put our trust in life and in death and whom we are to obey. Amen.

# Luke 1:46-55
## November 15, 1989
Bible Study at the Diocese Convent in Wittenberg

And Mary said,
My soul magnifies the Lord,
and my spirit rejoices in God my Savior,
for he has looked with favor on the lowliness
of his servant.
Surely, from now on all generations will
call me blessed;
for the Mighty One has done great things for me,
and holy is his name.
His mercy is for those who fear him
from generation to generation.
He has shown strength with his arm;
he has scattered the proud in the thoughts
of their hearts.
He has brought down the powerful from their
thrones, and lifted up the lowly,
he has filled the hungry with good things,
and sent the rich away empty.
He has helped his servant Israel, in remembrance
of his mercy,
according to the promise he made to our
ancestors, to Abraham and to his descendants
forever.

Knowing that this study would not be for men pastors but for women pastors, I searched a long time for a text for this Bible study. I knew that this day falls in the Decade for Peace, and it was clear to me that all of us would bring to this what is now happening in our country[27] and what is in our hearts. And the question is whether we are at all capable of listening to the text.

A few days ago it occurred to me that the Magnificat, Mary's hymn of praise, could be the biblical text for this hour. The Magnificat is the hymn of joy of a young woman. It has an unmistakable political tone, and in addition it has to do with Wittenberg: Luther dedicated his splendid commentary on the Magnificat to John Frederick, Duke of Saxony, in 1521. At that time Luther saw the theological and political relevance of this song to instructing the conscience of those in authority, while today we tend to focus more on lifting up the humbled.

In all likelihood Mary's song of joy belongs to the odes which, in addition to the Old Testament psalms and hymns, were sung in early Christian worship – such as Revelation 4:11; 5:9ff; 12:10f. This is not simply the lyric of a young girl nor the poem of a beautiful soul. Mary is not singing here a soprano solo, but rather in and with her sings the whole community of faith. She sings as the daughter of Zion.[28] Not only does the church listen to Mary as she sings, but it takes up the song of praise and sings with her. For the mercy that Mary praises is, to be sure, different for the church, but no less applicable than for her. Like Mary, the church is – if in a very different way – God's graciously chosen instrument which by the creative power of God's Spirit is prepared to "receive" the Savior and "proclaim him to the world."

Mary is praised by the church as being blessed (v. 48) because she believed (v. 45) and offered herself to the word in body and soul (v. 38). And also praised as being blessed are those who, like Mary, believe the word and hold fast to the word (Luke 11:27 f.). Once again, the whole community of faith sings with Mary and as one

---

[27] Translator's note: A week before this Bible study the Berlin Wall came down, symbolizing the "Wende", that is, the collapse of the GDR and the eventual reunification of the two Germanys.
[28] Translator's note: "Daughter of Zion" is an Old Testament reference to passages found in Isaiah, Jeremiah, Lamentations, Micah, Zephaniah, Zechariah, and some of the psalms. Later, Krusche will refer to "Zion-Mary".

with her. Luther says, "She sang it not for herself alone, but for us all, to sing it after her."[29]

It is a song with four stanzas which is now being tuned.

1st Stanza: Praise of God whose loftiness consists in taking the humbled into God's service.

To the one and only God, the Lord in the highest, who is above all and in all – to this God she opens her heart, to this God her soul joyfully soars, her song of joy is to this God. "My soul magnifies the Lord" – megalünein is the Greek word. "Great is the Lord," she cries out. That stands in stark contrast to the acclamations that are offered to the state gods (Acts 19:28, 34: "Great is Artemis of the Ephesians!" – for almost two hours the people cry out tumultuously in the city amphitheater.

Over against the megale-cries to state gods Mary set her megalünei which belongs to the God of Israel. The church, which sings with Mary and as she sings, cannot therefore chime in the praise songs that are sung to the other lords as if they brought salvation to the world. Wherever persons or powers are glorified as gods in hymns – where attributes such as "almighty" or "eternal" are conferred on them –, the church cannot join in. She must be silent. No, over against that she sings her song of praise to the glory of God in the highest, the Savior of the world. Not at all as a provocation, but as a quite obvious fact. Eventually, it will be a political statement of the first order.

When in the Soviet Union the personality cult was practiced and demanded bloody sacrifices, when the deification of the all-powerful party belonged to the pseudo-religious state cult, the Orthodox church continued to sing, unflinchingly, the doxology day after day, praising the Triune God, and by doing so forged a space in which the lowly were able to maintain their human dignity. They found their identity in praising God. In hymns of praise a church guards against fear of idols, and the singers are saved from fawning servility which so easily befalls the lowly. By singing to God they, as humbled persons, preserve their dignity.

---

[29] Translator's note: This quote is from Luther's commentary on the Magnificat which is found in Volume 21 of Luther's Works, p. 306 (Concordia Publishing House, 1956).

The basis for the songs of praise is precisely that God does not arrogantly ignore the powerless – as is customary among human beings –, that God also does not look down condescendingly on them and humiliates them, but rather he looks at them and confers respect on them: "for he has looked with favor on the lowliness of his servant." Those whom he has regarded he has also chosen.

The church sings praises with Mary to God in the highest because God works quite differently than the lords here on earth. The latter deal with people with whom they can make a deal – lofty finances, high intelligence, noble ancestry, physical prowess. God in the highest does not deal with the elite, but rather works with those who have nothing to offer. God calls into his service the small, the unimportant, the socially weak, the lowly, the humiliated, people without rank or name, those who do not count in the world, those of whom nothing is expected and who can make nothing of themselves. Precisely why them? Why us? Not because the small ones are better than the great ones, but rather because with people like us no one has the idea that God chooses particular persons – and certainly not the powerful in the world – based on wealth or intelligence or strength, but on spiritual innocence.

We are not exceptional people. It should be clear that it is God's issue, not ours. When God chose a people as instruments to deliver the world, God did not choose a politically powerful or culturally advanced people like the Egyptians or the Babylonians, but rather a small, insignificant nomadic people, a people that was of little consequence in the political world at the time (Deut. 7:7: "It was not because you were more numerous than any other people that the Lord...chose you, for you were the fewest of all peoples.")

This practice of choosing from below by God is continued in Mary. As God selected a young woman in such a way from his chosen people, a young woman who would bring the Messiah into the world, God did not choose someone from the upper ten thousand, but rather a modest, simple, unimportant girl, Mary. Luther writes: "This, therefore, is what Mary means: 'God has regarded me, a poor, despised, and lowly maiden, though He might have found a rich, renowned, noble, and mighty queen, the daughter of princes and great lords.... But He let His pure and gracious eyes light on me and used so poor and despised a maiden, in order that no one might glory in His presence, as though he were worthy of this, ...."[30]

This activity of God that goes against all worldly wisdom, to choose such a one to carry out God's acts of salvation history, ones who have nothing to recommend them, continues in choosing the church: when God called a community together that was supposed to bring into the world Mary's son, the Savior, God did not choose Greek philosophers or Roman patricians, but simple fishermen and rough dock workers, people without rank or name, without money or education, so that the apostle Paul can write, looking at the church, "not many of you were wise by human standards, not many were powerful, not many were of noble birth. But God chose what is foolish in the world to shame the wise; God chose what is weak in the world to shame the strong; God chose what is low and despised in the world, things that are not, to reduce to nothing things that are" (I Cor. 1:26ff.). And similarly in James: "Has not God chosen the poor in the world to be rich in faith...?" (James 2:5). And it is continued in the life of the early church: "Do not be haughty, but associate with the lowly" (Rom. 12:16). In the community of the God who chooses in such a way there cannot be a social climber mentality, but rather only solidarity with its weakest members, oriented to their possibilities and needs.

"You have looked with favor on the lowliness of your servant," Mary sings. You have chosen me, a low-regarded person who is not noticed by the world and therefore humbled. You have lifted up the humbled and chosen me, your unworthy servant made worthy, to bring the Savior into the world.

And now we may join Mary's hymn of praise: We thank you, God in the highest, that you have chosen us for your service, persons who do not count for much in the world and before you are completely unworthy. We have little to advise the world, but you wish to do something with us, namely, to proclaim the Savior to all the world. With that we can be useful to you by telling how Jesus enters our lives and makes us whole. That you want to have us! That you would risk that with us – and yet you know us so well!

---

[30] Translator's note: This quote is from Luther's commentary on the Magnificat which is found in Volume 21 of Luther's Works, p. 314 (Concordia Publishing House, 1956).

Lord, we praise you that our life is now worthwhile, even if no one else notices, even if our influence, our range of effectiveness is small. Our life is worthwhile even if one person experiences something of your love and discovers true joy.

Dear sisters, could you sing this? Or do you see this simply as an exaggeration? I can imagine some objections: Here the humility, the being from below, the being small or making oneself small is theologically elevated to a virtue. The humble attitude of service of the woman is glorified, her feeling of self-worth is minimized. Here the miserableness of the church, its elite-deficit, its marginal significance in world events is interpreted as God's will. Nietzsche wrote: "The Jews have brought off that miraculous feat of an inversion of values, thanks to which life on earth has acquired a novel and dangerous attraction for a couple of millennia: their prophets have fused 'rich,' 'godless,' 'evil,' 'violent,' and 'sensual' into one and were the first to use the word 'world' as an opprobrium. This inversion of values constitutes the significance of the Jewish people: they mark the beginning of the slave rebellion in morals."[31] In other words, the community of less value created value out of their lesser value. Because they are nothing, they explained, to be nothing was the proper understanding in God's eyes. To be such a poor, far from elite society became precisely the sign of being chosen.

I ask once again, Can and will you sing with Mary in view of the modest and often neglected service that you render in the church? Can you look at that work as something having to do with "bringing Jesus to the world," as something of which you are deemed worthy by God – or as something for which you will be condemned in the church? Can you begin something that your reputation depends on being seen and chosen by God – or is that a theologically, perhaps correct, statement, but one that is not grounded in experience and cannot become one's experience?

"My soul magnifies the Lord" – a statement of experience? Or does it seem, regrettably, to offer no joy? Are we capable of praising God for such an absolutely unexceptional, poor church that is unqualified, according to worldly standards, and to thank

---

[31] Translator's Note: In Beyond Good & Evil (Passage #195, p. 108), Translated by Walter Kaufmann, (Random House, 1966).

God for it? Is it difficult for us to believe that it could be chosen to present the Savior to the world? Have we ever given thanks to God for the church?

2nd Stanza: Song of praise to God who will be forever merciful to us (v. 49-50).

The "great things" (the megala) that God has done to Mary are that God chose her to receive and present to the world the Messiah and thereby usher in the crucial salvation-historical time in which God's great deeds (Acts 2:11) will occur and be proclaimed.

What especially propels the praise of mercy is that it is not one that arises from a temporary, momentary emotion of the divine heart and then retreats again, but instead it is a fundamental, lasting mercy that is intended for everyone – "from generation to generation" – because it is part of God's innermost being. God's "holy name." What happens to Mary and that for which she is chosen is nothing exceptional, but something exemplary. It is part of the continuum of divine demonstrations of mercy.

Mary knows that God's merciful aspect was not simply a moment of mercy, but rather "God's mercy extending from generation to generation." With Mary's son God's great compassion is exhibited to this merciless and therefore wretched world – forever. Now everyone can appeal to it and cry out in their fear, guilt, distress, and hopelessness. "Lord, have mercy on me!" And the church, as the voice of the world in the face of its cry of misery to heaven, may pray the Kyrie eleison.

"God's mercy extends from generation to generation" – it is enough. For our children and for their children. God's compassion is not simply at the end of the day, but it is fresh every morning. Fresh and new. From generation to generation – and never stale, but always natural.

3rd Stanza: Praising the God who carries out the eschatological change in relationship and takes on our fear of the powerful.

Zion-Mary sings praise to the God who is merciful and who, because God is merciful, does not stand by idly when power is exercised mercilessly, but sets in motion the eschatological change in relationships: "He has shown strength with his arm; he has scattered the proud in the thoughts of their hearts. He has brought down the powerful from their thrones, and lifted up the lowly."

Mary had it hard enough to have to experience power being exercised mercilessly. The imperial order to be registered for tax purposes forced her in her advanced pregnancy to make the difficult journey to Bethlehem. How important are the difficulty and danger for a woman when an emperor needs money? And then she had to escape under cover of darkness with her infant as a precaution because a suspicious king was having two year old boys liquidated. What does a human life mean, the pain of a few mothers, when security of power is at stake? And finally, Mary must stand at the foot of the cross and watch as her son is put to death because the judge, convinced of the innocence of the accused, did not want to risk angering his superiors.

In the face of her own experiences of powerlessness she praises God. She has to come to terms with those experiences. With her exaltation from lowliness the eschatological inversion of relationship began, and with it God's assault with robust compassion on the ostensibly stable status quo of human hubris, complacent and unmerciful use of political (v. 52) and economic (v. 53) power. Not because they have power, but rather because they use it ruthlessly, because they treat people condescendingly, because they scorn, humiliate, walk over, and violate people, God sweeps them away and throws them down from the platforms of their power.

Illustrations of the third stanza can be found throughout world history with the rise and fall of rulers even in recent times (Hitler, Mussolini, Stalin, the Shah of Iran, Ferdinand Marcos, to name only a few). This is not to demonize power and its use – the church, as it sings with Mary does not say, "Power is evil," but it also does not say sweepingly, "Power does evil things." Zion-Mary is no chaotic anarchist. Luther writes, "Observe, however, that Mary does not say He breaks the seats, but He casts the mighty from their seats.... For while the world stands, authority, rule, power, and seats must remain. But God will not long permit men to abuse them and turn them against Him, inflict injustice and violence on the godly, ...."[32]

With that the issue for Luther – the commentary is aimed at a governmental official – is that misuse of power takes place by someone in the institutions of power, while today we see more clearly that the institutions themselves are often enough institutionalized misuse of power. Luther, however, is correct to point out that power and the exercise of power are necessary in this world. The Magnificat says nothing at all about outlawing authority which would lead to anarchy. Neither is there here a philosophy of powerless people who in their weakness dream of escaping their misery as they see the upper crust being brought down and the least becoming strong, and they being able to occupy the empty throne and assuming seats of power.

That God raises up the lowly (v. 52) does not mean that the weak will rise and fill the power positions of the authorities. That would accomplish little. The eschatological radical change is different from all revolutions heretofore in that here not simply do oppressor and oppressed change places, that is, a revolution of relationships succeeds without a change of heart. That God raises up the lowly, as God raised the humbled Christ, means that God shares power with them, that God decisively includes them in ruling through their prayers, their witness to the truth, their own conversion and call to change course, their active anticipation of the kingdom, and through living justly. Not the mean-spirited gloating over the demise of the arrogant and power hungry, but great joy that the despondent and humiliated are lifted up and are learning to walk with dignity. "You lift up the lowly," Zion-Mary sings: You allow the powerless to participate in your kingdom which is marked not by the image of clinched fists, but by the image of the pierced hands which bear the signature of the cross.

"You lift up the lowly" does not simply mean that you place them in positions of power, but that you share part of your kingdom with them. When God shares with them the exercise of political power, then those whom God has lifted up will never again

---

[32] Translator's note: This quote is from Luther's commentary on the Magnificat which is found in Volume 21 of Luther's Works, p. 344 (Concordia Publishing House, 1956).

humiliate others or have others humiliated, but they will take care that those whom God loves and has called to live in the splendid freedom of God's children come to God's justice, no longer as diminished persons.

Those whom God has lifted up from their lowliness, participants in God's rule, must know that the eschatological radical change, the eschatological revolution, the realization of the kingdom in which all lowliness, all injustice, all hunger, all weeping will be done away with. This will not be accomplished by us because what we can achieve, even in the best case, will be only a weak reflection of what God has promised and will bring to fruition. That should not deter, but rather inspire us to do what is possible and necessary here, that which corresponds to the coming kingdom. But we must guard against letting disappointment and fruitlessness set us back which might tempt us to give up. The hymn of praise is to that one who makes all things new, who is the Alpha and Omega, who was at the beginning and who will bring creation to its completion, who protects his church from decline into resignation and makes it into a calm resistance movement against hopelessness.

What does it mean for the world if in the midst of great songs of praise to oneself, hateful songs are lifted up against others, mournful songs of those who have given up, what does it mean in the midst of all that for the church to praise God in song and to exhibit that joy in its life – I think that is difficult to measure.

The church that praises God in song, that fills the hungry with good things, will not be silent or speak in vague terms even if it means incurring the wrath of those in power or jeopardizing its position in society. Luther writes: "Unbelief means that we see God's Word, the truth, and the right defeated and wrong triumph and remain silent, do not rebuke, speak out or prevent it, but let things go as they will.... We are afraid that we, too, might be attacked and made poor and might then perish of hunger and be forever laid low."[33]

4th Stanza: Praise the God who honors his own word (v. 54-55).

---

[33] Translator's note: This quote is from Luther's commentary on the Magnificat which is found in Volume 21 of Luther's Works, p. 347 (Concordia Publishing House, 1956).

In the choice of Mary, Israel, the despised and abused servant of God (Isaiah 41:8), is lifted up and exalted. What takes place in and with Mary is the fulfillment event toward which the entire story of covenant and promise up to now points. God remembers, as it were, all the promises of compassion made to the fathers – God remembers (Psalm 98:3) – and they are made real in this story. With the birth of the Messiah God fulfills the prayers, hopes, and expectations of the humbled, enslaved people of God. Israel did not wait, pray, or hope in vain.

It seems clear to me that we can sing the Magnificat only with Israel, that is, together with the people of the promises, not as the church which has inherited Israel and thus disinherited Israel and sees Israel as without promise. Today Jews can join in singing the Magnificat only insofar as they see in Mary's son their brother Jesus whom God has given them, but not as the promised Messiah.

In part, that is the fault of Christendom. Pinchas Lapide wrote to Hans Küng: "For 1800 years the church has done three things with Jesus: it has de-Judaized him, it has Hellenized him, and it has very effectively spoiled him for all of us: through threatening sermons, threatening baptisms, through kidnapping – the rest you know as well as I."[34]

I believe we must allow the Jews time to discover Jesus in whose name they have had to suffer acts of humiliation and inhumanity, as their brother for whom they have waited. He has another function for them as well as for the non-Jew, namely, he leads the latter to the God whom they did not know before, and he leads the Jews back to the well-known God of their fathers. For them he is the renewer of the Torah covenant, for the Gentiles he becomes the founder of a new covenant with the God of Israel.

In any case, we have in common with the Jews the hope for the kingdom of God. They are waiting for the coming of the Messiah, and we await the Parousia – the final coming of the Lord. With that, it is clear to us that the Messiah expected by the Jews will bear the characteristics of Jesus Christ. On the common path which we travel with each other, albeit separately, into the future of our

---

[34] Translator"s note: Pinchas Lapide, a Jewish theologian and Israeli historian and diplomat (1922-1997); Hans Küng, a Swiss Roman Catholic priest and theologian (born 1928). Quotation from Lapide is my translation.

common God, we can still sing the Magnificat together, even with a different understanding, and praise God as that one who is true to his word, and leave to him whatever he makes of this shared praise. We must begin there.

# Luke 10:17-20
## October 19, 1988
### Sermon on at the Mission Bible School in Malche near Freienwalde[35]

The seventy returned with joy, saying, "Lord, in your name even the demons submit to us!" He said to them, "I watched Satan fall from heaven like a flash of lightning. See, I have given you authority to tread on snakes and scorpions, and over all the power of the enemy; and nothing will hurt you. Nevertheless, do not rejoice at this, that the spirits submit to you, but rejoice that your names are written in heaven.

Dear Sisters and Brothers! The church that belongs to Jesus the Victor has every reason to rejoice. It is important that with everything about which you rejoice the actual, the crucial, basis for joy that underlies it all is not overlooked. "Do not rejoice that the spirits submit to you, but rejoice that your names are written in heaven." With this prohibition is the joy of experiences carried out by the power of Jesus' name to be rejected as false or illegitimate? I think not. Experiences can justifiably lead to joy, but they are not the basis for joy. Joy that depended on experience would be dangerous if it came at the expense of the joy that is grounded in being chosen. It is not simply a matter of being chosen versus experience. The relative importance of experience is not to be disputed. However, gracious election comes before any and all significant experiences – of that Jesus leaves no doubt.

The church that belongs to Jesus the Victor should know:

1. Experience of the liberating power of Jesus Christ – that is important.

2. Assurance of gracious election – that is crucial.

---

[35] Translator's note: a small town about 60 km (40 miles) northeast of Berlin. The Protestant school was founded in 1898, originally intended only for girls. Later, the school included men as well. The theological aspect of education there ended in 2011.)

I.

Experience of the liberating power of Jesus – that is important.

It is the joy of missionaries that is being reported here. They return from their evangelistic efforts and report to Jesus everything they have experienced. They did not keep his name for themselves, not only uttering it among themselves, but they were entrusted with the name of Jesus and had gone out in his name where no one had heard of him. They had set out armed with his word. "See, I am sending you out like lambs into the midst of wolves" (Lk. 10:3), he had said to them. With that Jesus was not intending to prejudge those to whom he was sending his disciples, but rather he was wanting to say to his disciples, I am sending you as messengers of my peace. You may not either threaten the people or make them anxious – lambs do not bare their teeth to wolves. Not only may you not, but neither should you. You go out as messengers of my unarmed and vulnerable love. You are to deliver a joyful message, not a threatening one. Jesus expects his own to go unarmed and peacefully into truly unpredictable situations (lambs among wolves!). He does not expect them to remain in their stall where it is nice and warm and they are with each other. Instead, he demands that they risk encountering others on their own terrifying turf.

They had accepted this challenge in trust, venturing out where Jesus' name was not known and engaging others about him. And now they were reporting on their visits and conversations. What was it like to be lambs among wolves? Did they expect something different than to return having been attacked, intimidated, made to feel anxious, beaten, and to report how they had been pursued, assaulted, and ridiculed? There was not a hint of that in their report. "They returned with joy, saying, 'Lord, in your name even the demons submit to us!'" They had amazing experiences with the power of Jesus' name – they, these unarmed people. I imagine their announcement of success was not brief, but they probably went into great detail about what happened as they told of their encounters, that in Jesus God's kingdom had dawned, that he frees people from their guilt, inhibitions, and fears, and gives them a new life.

I do not believe that they told sensational tales of driving out demons. The realm of the occult is certainly not the particular domain of demons. There are many more evil spirits, more everyday ghosts that frighten people, forces that enslave people, tormentors that torture people, phantoms that dupe them.

Today the reports might sound something like this: In a parent assembly at school it was said that we should hate our enemies and so raise our children. Then we said that we would like to point to Jesus to whom we and our children belong! He did not hate his enemies, but loved them, and we want to follow that example. When we said that, the spirit of fear to which the people had succumbed and which they had already inculcated in their children, noticeably softened: Don't say what you are thinking, but rather what they want to hear! When we had mentioned Jesus' name, it suddenly became quite still, and then the parents began to talk and speak freely how it really is. When we mentioned your name, Lord, the spell of speechlessness was simply broken.

Perhaps someone would say, I participated in the Olaf Palme Peace March.[36] I walked behind the cross that someone up ahead carried, but we were not on a crusade against the Communists. We walked with them. When we stopped, we went into the church and prayed. They remained outside. When we resumed, conversations began. They wanted to know what the cross meant. We talked about you, Lord, how from the cross you prayed for your executioners and how from the cross you made peace between God and us. They listened. The evil spirit of intransigence and obstinacy did not arise. It had no chance.

The report of two others might be something like this. We cared for one who was an alcoholic. His digs looked like – forgive us, Lord – a pigsty. The first thing we did was to clean it up. Then we asked him if he wanted to be free. Yes, he said, I have tried several times, but it has never worked. Then we told him about you, how you have freed people who no longer had a will of their own. We visited him every day and continued to tell him about you. We took

---

[36] Translator's note: This was a peace march that took place in the GDR in September 1987. People from the BRD and Czechoslovakia also took part. Olaf Palme was a Swedish prime minister from 1969-1976 and was assassinated on February 28,1986.

him to work and picked him up from work. We took him with us to a youth group meeting (they looked at him stunned) and prayed for him. Today he has been dry for several months. We are praying that he makes it.

Now some of you, no doubt, could report what you have recently experienced with the name of Jesus. I am sure you could, even if you don't think so, tell of grand, spectacular things. I could not report any either. However, perhaps you were able to please someone by singing and drive away the spirit of sadness or bitterness. Or perhaps you were able to help someone who was anxious before an exam or an operation, so that they no longer felt the threat of this torment.

It is the triumph of Christ that makes possible such freedom and obtains it for them. Jesus' word about the downfall of Satan – "I watched Satan fall from heaven like a flash of lightning" – wants to say, The power of the adversary is fundamentally broken. That is an indisputable fact that can never be retracted. The lightning is over and can never return. To me, Jesus says, the adversary and enemy of people has come to nothing. Whoever follows me comes under my rule.

At the same time Jesus wants to say to us, The power of the accuser is broken. He has been driven out of heaven and cannot return. There is no place for him there. No longer is there anyone there who can hold up to God your doubtful names and your failures. No longer can anyone appear against you because I will intercede for you. No longer do you need to obsess and be paralyzed by accusations and rebukes that others raise against you: "Who will bring any charge against God's elect? Christ is here" (Rom. 8:33).

The triumph over the devil not only made possible the experiences of the apostles, but it especially gave them courage for bold ventures. Ultimately, Jesus makes his people unassailable: "I have given you authority to tread on snakes and scorpions, and over all the power of the enemy; and nothing will hurt you." We may walk our path without fear. It is a dangerous path. "Our ancient foe" is defeated, but he does not give up. "His craft and power are great; and armed with cruel hate."[37]

The apostles know that dangers lie in wait all around them: hidden, intangible, furtive, insidious, suddenly appearing before them and bearing poisonous teeth – like snakes – but Jesus' people must not anxiously imagine what could be lurking there. They must not carefully creep along the ground, but instead they move freely forward unconcerned – "See, I have given you authority to tread on snakes and scorpions." All poison splattered against them, any bites they may receive, any stings that may be inflicted on them will prove to be harmless. We are not spared everything, but we will not die from them. We are the community that belongs to Jesus the victor. Experience of the liberating power of Jesus – that is important.

II.

Assurance of gracious election – that is crucial.

We can and may have experiences with the strength of Jesus' name, experiences in which we may justifiably rejoice. But they are not decisive. What is crucial is not what may have happened in Jesus' name. What is crucial is God's gracious election without our doing a thing. "Do not rejoice at this, that the spirits submit to you, but rejoice that your names are written in heaven."

Why shouldn't we rejoice that through the efforts of Christians paralysis and fear and depression are overcome, mistrust is dismantled, fanaticism and irreconcilability are removed, passions and narrow-mindedness are reduced, and thus the evil, destructive, misanthropic spirits are driven out. Why shouldn't we rejoice at all this?

Perhaps it is because that kind of joy so easily becomes conceit – we have experienced that. We must only place ourselves at the absolute service of the Lord, and then we experience something.

---

[37] Translator's note: from Martin Luther's hymn "A Mighty Fortress Is Our God".

We are the plenipotentiaries of Christ. We think that with its dearth of spiritual experiences the church has little to offer us. In order to grow spiritually we must separate ourselves from her and establish our own communities. Because Jesus saw this spiritual arrogance coming, the selfish attention on one's own experiences – hence his warning.

I can think of another reason Jesus suppressed the understandable joy of his messengers. If the joy is based on such experiences, what happens when such experiences fail to produce results? When failures, disappointments, defeats come? When, in spite of costly and tireless labor, one sees the flock become smaller and smaller, and the children stay away? When in the face of a sermon on the kingdom of God the spirit of fear does not give way, but harden hearts even more, so that they no longer dare to let their children go to Sunday school? When the word of reconciliation falls on deaf ears and only causes more harm and injury? When charismatic uprisings, which began so nicely, lead to arrogance and divisions? When I hear no mention of the power of Jesus' name and at the same time hear others report of their triumphs? Must that not lead to an internal collapse?

Jesus wants to say this: Rejoice that you do not depend on your experiences and on what you have seen and accomplished. Be glad that you do not have to prove that you belong to him by having a catalogue of victorious deeds, but that you are confirmed as belonging to him by means of your name being entered in the book of the covenant of grace. No one's name is there because they had a dramatic experience, and no name is stricken because they cannot point to any such experience. The basis for your joy is not whatever you have done, but rather God's incomprehensible election. Not by virtue of anything you have done on earth, but what has happened for you in heaven. Our joy over the demise of Satan consists not in the possible breeches in his rule, but in the protests against our names that have been silenced.

Our names – and that means we as persons and our whole life story – are real to God, preserved in God's memory. Our names are in God's mind and will never be lost. They will never be forgotten, even when no one on earth will remember us.

Dear sisters and brothers, rejoice that you are inscribed in the lamb's book of life. Satan has been cast out of heaven. The power of the brothers' accuser is broken. There is no longer anyone there who can last before God or who can raise doubts about your name. Your burdened and slandered name, your misused and forgotten name stands in good stead. It stands in good stead because it is written with the blood of Christ, inscribed in God's heart, preserved in God's eternal memory. Our names are also kept elsewhere. In some computer. There also are dates fed into it, especially those that burden us. Our name in the computer can be erased. No one can ever erase the good name we have with God. The Lord will call us by this name on the great resurrection day.

"Nevertheless, do not rejoice at this, that the spirits submit to you, but rejoice that your names are written in heaven." That is said only to those who have been entrusted with the name of Jesus. For the others who only wanted to enjoy the safety of a warm sheepfold, this word from Jesus would frankly be poison because it would confirm their joy in being chosen without having to deal with the evil spirits. This word is only for those who get on with the journey. Among them are also those who in their own judgment have nothing to show for their efforts. Would not the Lord say to them: Announcements of victory are not important, but rather what's important is that you belong to Christ. And he fought that battle on the cross where everything appeared to be lost. In other respects, how do you know whether or not there was some spiritual confusion that had to be erased without being able to register you? That we belong to the crucified victor without having had to point to our experiences is the firm basis of our joy. To belong to him: we don't have any more, we don't need any more, and there isn't any more. No one can take this joy from us. Amen.

# Luke 24:13-35
## June 8, 1986
2nd Sunday after Trinity Sunday in Kassel-Kirchditmold[38] – worship service at the regional Kirchentag

Now on that same day two of them were going to a village called Emmaus, about seven miles from Jerusalem, and talking with each other about all these things that had happened. While they were talking and discussing, Jesus himself came near and went with them, but their eyes were kept from recognizing him. And he said to them, "What are you discussing with each other while you walk along?" They stood still, looking sad. Then one of them, whose name was Cleopas, answered him, "Are you the only stranger in Jerusalem who does not know the things that have taken place there in these days?" He asked them, "What things?" They replied, "The things about Jesus of Nazareth, who was a prophet mighty in deed and word before God and all the people, and how our chief priests and leaders handed him over to be condemned to death and crucified him. But we had hoped that he was the one to redeem Israel. Yes, and besides all this, it is now the third day since these things took place. Moreover, some women of our group astounded us. They were at the tomb early this morning, and when they did not find his body there, they came back and told us that they had indeed seen a vision of angels who said that he was alive. Some of those who were with us went to the tomb and found it just as the women had said; but they did not see him." Then he said to them, "Oh, how foolish you are, and how slow of heart to believe all that the prophets have declared! Was it not necessary that the Messiah should suffer these things and then enter into his glory?" Then beginning with Moses and all the prophets, he interpreted to them the things about himself in all the Scriptures.

As they came near the village to which they were going, he walked ahead as if he were going on. But they urged him strongly, saying, "Stay with us, because it is almost evening and the day is now

---

[38] Translator's note: Kassel is a city that was in West Germany. Ditmold is a suburb of Kassel.

nearly over." So he went in to stay with them. When he was at the table with them, he took bread, blessed and broke it, and gave it to them. Then their eyes were opened, and they recognized him; and he vanished from their sight. They said to each other, "Were not our hearts burning within us while he was talking to us on the road, while he was opening the Scriptures to us?" That same hour they got up and returned to Jerusalem; and they found the eleven and their companions gathered together. They were saying, "The Lord has risen indeed, and he has appeared to Simon!" Then they told what had happened on the road, and how he had been made known to them in the breaking of the bread.

Dear Friends! Luke tells us a road trip story. Two persons travel together on the road, on life's road. They are not only walking with each other, but they are engaged in a conversation. They are not traveling independently of each other, but something is stirring within them. They need each other to try to work it out. Without a conversation partner, without a travel companion, without sharing thoughts and feelings, without open hearts, things would be bleak.

The two friends or brothers who are part of this story – we do know them; it could just as easily have been a husband and wife or a small group – have something in common with each other, namely, a shared experience. They came into contact with Jesus who infected them – infected them with a great hope. They had seen how he attacked human misery and its wretchedness and transformed them, signaling in him God's coming rule. Through him everything would be different. And now the one on whom they had hung all their hopes had been hung. When they saw him strung up on the cross, their hopes were dashed. Now everything would stay as it is. Nothing would change. And that's why they were returning to their hometown where they would now have to continue to live with their unrealized hope.

"But we had hoped...," they say. I think we know that sentiment: We hoped that our children would one day walk the way of faith. – We hoped that Jesus would protect our marriage from having deep disappointments – We hoped that our own life in communion with Jesus would become more radiant, more convincing, happier. – We hoped that our churches would be changed, that our congregation would become more active.

Perhaps the disappointed hope of the two disciples especially today would be in those who, infected by Jesus, stood up against the relentless arms race, risking themselves and experiencing complete powerlessness. Their warnings having gone unheeded, rockets were installed and went unchecked. "But we hoped," we would be able to stop the madness. We were aroused and inspired by him, the Prince of Peace. And now we have nothing to show for our efforts. Everything goes on as before.

How many of those who once looked to Jesus full of expectations, who were promised much by him for their personal life and for the life of the world, would like to have walked the road of those two disciples – away from the others, tired, resigned, drained, extremely disappointed –, the road to their Emmaus, the place from which they had set out and where they would have to live with their buried hope. A life without any perspective.

But these two are not there yet. They are still on the road with each other. This serious story tells us that their journey does not end in Emmaus, but rather it ends where it had started and where they met Jesus and had been infected with hope by him. Their journey ends in Jerusalem, in the community of the disciples from which they had run away because it did not seem worth their while to stay.

The road to Emmaus was a detour. There are healthy, essential detours, roads that must be taken in order to experience something new, detours to reach a goal. Paul needs to take a detour on the road to Damascus, the Ethiopian treasurer takes a detour to Jerusalem to reach a goal, namely, to have a vital experience with the living Christ. Not all detours are wrong ways or dead-ends that result in emptiness. It leaves us hoping for the living touch of Jesus, but now we find ourselves on a road on which the abyss between us and him has only grown deeper. It could very well be a detour which they must take because otherwise they would have landed in the sterility and petrification of theological formulas or biblical literal correctness, and become dried up.

The story of these two disciples has this to say to us: When two persons who are with each other on life's way begin to talk with each other, when they confess to each other how difficult faith is for them, how much has become doubtful or shattered, how uncertain they are about many things, how little there is of Jesus in their life, that is a healthy step because they are no longer trying to manage everything by themselves, but instead have someone with whom they can discuss, think, and ponder everything, someone who walks beside them and remains at their side and who is not always a few steps ahead and has an answer for everything.

Above all, from this road trip story we should understand that wherever persons who have in some way come into contact with Jesus who takes an interest in their disappointments and confusion, then he is already with them and listens to them before they are aware of it and without recognizing who he is. And he makes them comfortable enough to share their concerns. Not only do they not need to hide their skeptical, disappointed, doubting thoughts from each other, but they do not need to conceal them from him. They don't need to act as if the news of the empty grave and the message that the one who was crucified is alive has taken away their doubt. They can honestly say – as the two do, in fact, say here – that the empty grave proves nothing at all to them.

The Lord who walks with them unrecognized on the road does not remove their doubt – but neither does he praise them for expressing their intellectual honesty – rather, he brings Scripture into the conversation.

The Scriptures, whose expositor and whose interpretation he is, become for all who have walked this road the indispensable conversation partner. In the back and forth between one's own experience and the word of Scripture – in this moment comes illumination, insights, understanding, perspective, assurances which revive the heart and simply make one happy. "Were not our hearts burning within us while he was talking to us on the road, while he was opening the scriptures to us?" the two say.

As is true for everyone who has Scripture and the Lord speaking through it as a conversation partner, their minds were opened to the fact that God and suffering belong together, that God decided for the way of the cross. That's not what the two disciples wanted – and neither do we – that God did not take the path of power and success, but rather the path of powerlessness and failure, and thereby reach the goal. "But we had hoped that he was the one to redeem Israel," the two disappointed disciples had said. Not that their hope was misplaced – their hope was by no means in vain –, but instead that they were unable to bring their hope together with the cross, that they saw the cross as the end and the refutation of their hope.

They had to learn, over and over again, as we must also, to grasp that God does not take the path of power which tramples down all opposition, but rather the path of love which suffers and overcomes the opposition; that God does not sacrifice the world for himself, but sacrifices himself for the world; that God does not charge us with being guilty, but rather takes our guilt on himself and removes it from the world. Because that is the only way the world can be helped, because that is the only way the destructive law of mutual assignment of guilt and reciprocal threats – blow answered by counter- blow, measure answered by counter-measure, demand answered with counter-demand – can be overcome. In this profound sense the suffering of Christ was necessary. "Was it not necessary that the Messiah should suffer these things and then enter into his glory?"

When persons consider their experiences and listen to Scripture and are open to the Lord speaking through it of something of the mystery of the cross, they have reached a very profound, if not the essential, insight. To them it becomes then clear that the way of Jesus and thus also our own cannot be a smooth one. "Was it not necessary that the Messiah should suffer?" That sounds so logical, so obvious. But the reality was not at all so smooth. He who had announced to his disciples, "The Son of man must suffer much," prays in the Garden of Gethsemane, "Abba, Father, ...let this cup pass from me (spare me suffering); yet not what I want but what you want" (Mt. 26:39). The suffering is not taken away in some fatalistic way because it has to happen, but instead here we have resistance and surrender.[39] He whose future meant resurrection

---

[39] Translator's note: The German here is "Widerstand und Ergebung" which Krusche surely knew was the title to a book by Dietrich Bonhoeffer who engaged in the resistance movement against Hitler in World War II and was executed in the Flossenbürg concentration camp shortly before the end of the war. The English title of Bonhoeffer's book is Letters and Papers from Prison.

confronted the suffering of death with fear and trembling and nevertheless accepted it.

Those two disciples on the road, and we also, must learn from this road trip story: Our hope in God and God's rule, in Christ and his future is a hope that must go through the cross – through setbacks, disappointments, failures, temptations – but a hope that cannot be refuted. The crucified hope cannot control the future, but it holds fast to it. By the cross hope is liberated to align one's own expectations with God's future and to cling irrevocably to the hoped for outcome.

With this understanding we are not at all through. We do not have that hope once and for all. It must be prayed for again and again, and received fresh each day.

The request of the two disciples to the stranger, about whom so far they were more suspicious than knowledgeable, was "Stay with us!" This is the legitimation for the prayers of all inquirers and seekers. Non-believers may invite him. The prayer is not the privilege of the pious.

When persons – two or more – set out on a shared journey, prayer has an overriding significance. "Stay with us" – he will not remain alone, and we do not want to be alone in the evening as the day is coming to an end and night is approaching. Again, we know what that can mean: It could be the evening of the world, it could be a difficult night ahead, the night of unimaginable horror, the last night. We do not want to surrender to this night, submitting to the impenetrable and sinister, to the powers of darkness. That is a prayer against the fear of the future and for keeping hope alive. Thus, a prayer that Christ did not leave the world to its own devices, but rather wanted to remain devoted to it.

The fulfillment of this request is reflected in the common meal – in the words of thanksgiving, the breaking and sharing of the bread. It then becomes clear to them and there can be no more doubt: It is **He! He**, the crucified one. **He**, away from whose community they had run. The exact same words are used here that Jesus had spoken to his disciples on the evening before his crucifixion as they shared the meal with each other. Naturally, Luke wants us to remember: The table where the bread is broken, blessed, and shared is the table of the Lord. He is present there, the crucified one who is risen; there those who question, seek, and ask become aware and certain of his presence. There they discover one another as part of his community. They are not alone. There the sense of resignation is overcome, there they begin to live a new life.

Of course, his presence cannot be captured. "Then their eyes were opened, and they recognized him; and he vanished from their sight." We cannot preserve the certainty of his presence. It will be made new again and again, with each new encounter with Scripture, with each new approach to the Lord's table. We are not to live simply by one experience, but must be open to fresh new experiences, again and again, on our journey.

The two do not stay in Emmaus. There's no thought given here to slipping back into a life that has lost perspective. Those to whom the Lord has disclosed the mystery of the cross, and those whom in an hour of darkness he meets at his table with the gift of his presence, they are renewed again, and they go to others for whom, like them, hope had begun to die and who now must experience the risen one who had been crucified. The community of the road becomes the community of witnesses.

And therein the two experience something most noteworthy: The others already know everything. The two who returned want to report to the others their overwhelming experience, but they learn from them that they have already had a similar experience. Before the two can say anything, others exclaim to them, "The Lord has risen indeed."

Perhaps we also have experienced something like that. We are prepared to tell others of our experience only to discover that they have had an experience with Christ, if not one perhaps as powerful as that of the eleven disciples. Sometimes surprising experiences take place when groups get together in which normally we hear only political cliches, and then discover an experience of Christ which we had never expected from them. And it will be good if things happen as in this story, that we not begin with our experiences, but rather that they come first to the Word and tell how the living Christ encountered them and what they learned from him and what that kindled in them. Then they will surely be prepared also to hear our story in which Scripture and prayer and the Lord's Supper will have an important place.

The encounter with persons whom the living Christ has also already met is always one of joy. And now as fellow-travelers we shall share the common experience in his meal. All is prepared. He is there for us with his whole life. He pours out for us the cup of life to the end. And he lays on our heart those who know nothing yet of this life. Amen.

# John 5:1-18
## October 16, 1977
### 19th Sunday after Trinity Sunday in the Cathedral at Magdeburg

After this there was a festival of the Jews, and Jesus went up to Jerusalem.

Now in Jerusalem by the Sheep Gate there is a pool, called in Hebrew Bethzatha, which has five porticoes. In these lay many invalids – blind, lame, and paralyzed. One man was there who had been ill for thirty-eight years. When Jesus saw him lying there and knew that he had been there a long time, he said to him, "Do you want to be made well?" The sick man answered him, "Sir, I have no one to put me into the pool when the water is stirred up; and while I am making my way, someone else steps down ahead of me." Jesus said to him, "Stand up, take your mat and walk." At once the man was made well, and he took up his mat and began to walk.

Now that day was a sabbath. So the Jews said to the man who had been cured, "It is the sabbath; it is not lawful for you to carry your mat." But he answered them, "The man who made me well said to me, 'Take up your mat and walk.'" They asked him, "Who is the man who said to you, 'Take it up and walk'?" Now the man who had been healed did not know who it was, for Jesus had disappeared in the crowd that was there. Later Jesus found him in the temple and said to him, "See, you have been made well! Do not sin any more, so that nothing worse happens to you." The man went away and told the Jews that it was Jesus who had made him well. Therefore the Jews started persecuting Jesus, because he was doing such things on the sabbath. But Jesus answered them, "My Father is still working, and I also am working." For this reason the Jews were seeking all the more to kill him, because he was not only breaking the sabbath, but was also calling God his own Father, thereby making himself equal to God.

Dear Friends! Sometimes I play a game with my radio. At news time I turn the knob without looking for a particular station. If I come across a German voice, I try to determine where it's coming from. Normally, it doesn't take more than ten seconds before it is clear. When there is news of a crisis or some exciting announcement, the source is clear. When announcements of success and optimism are beamed, the point of origin is also clear.

Somewhere between the images of horror and images of the ideal is reality, that which we perceive with our own eyes and ears and process with our own mind. That which we absorb daily in strange images and news reports and what we ourselves observe and experience is not likely to arouse grand hopes. The daily experience of reality is not usually associated with matters of hope. People have come to mistrust optimistic prognoses and ideological models of the future. If in spite of everything we Christians have any hope for the world, it is not because we had created better experiences for the world, but it's because through Jesus Christ we know this: God does not leave the creation to its own wretchedness, but instead sets it right. "My Father is still working, and I also am working," Jesus says here. God is undeterred at work. God sees the world not simply as new, as philosophers do, and God does not simply change it, as revolutionaries do, but God sets it right, makes it whole. Since God in Jesus Christ entered the reality of our world and accepted it, the world gained a future and human life gained meaning.

In the scene which is described here something of that becomes evident as he, as the Savior of the world, is at work, and we can therefore rely on him.

1. He associates with the lonely

2. He frees him from his miserable paralysis.

3. He makes him the unmistakable sign of the dawn of the salvific future.

I.

Jesus associates with the lonely.

A great festival is being celebrated in the capital city of the country. We know what that is like. Whether it is informal and calls for shirtsleeves or more official that is more intimate and calls for good taste, all festivals have one thing in common, namely, there are those who participate, the fortunate ones who enjoy success, and then there are those who cannot celebrate, who are alone with their sadness, their illness, their life's burdens. Between the two there is a massive chasm.

Jesus does not go inside to the festival, but goes instead to those who are excluded from it. He does not go to the fairgrounds or into the festival hall, but to the hospital where all of human misery is crouched together in a heap. He does not begrudge the celebrants their enjoyment and does not pass judgment on their festival. But his thoughts were with those who cannot join the celebration and, with that, he poses a question for all celebrations as to whether they are not a deception because the celebration is only possible if and as one overlooks, shields, rises above, distances oneself from human misery. People in wheelchairs, with crutches, with disfigured faces, with distressed looks, and pitiful clothing do not fit the decor. They ruin the atmosphere, and are embarrassing reminders of the world's misery which one would just as soon forget.

A true festival is one in which all may take part and from which no one is excluded. Indeed, those who think that wherever the miserable are concentrated together, it is better since one finds more humanity there than where the carefree and happy celebrate their festival, are simply wrong. Misery as such never has promoted solidarity. It does not automatically bring about a community of suffering and assistance, but rather alarmingly it fosters the ruthless competition of selfish survival. There are the medicinal waters, the forms of misery encamped all around.

When the springs bubble up and the water from the pool is stirred up, one can always go in. But only one. One at a time can race in. Naturally, the most robust who pushed past the others was able to be first. In this story the rule seems to be: "You are always next in line" and "Nice guys finish last." Vae victis – Woe to the vanquished, the tossed aside, those trampled to the ground.

Into this world in which the strong, healthy, and beautiful exclude the weak and unsightly from the festival and in which there is a ruthless struggle among the weak for the best places that have access to the pool, Jesus enters. Unbidden, unexpected, unnoticed. The people enjoying their own party are happy enough. And those outside the party expect help from the medicinal waters. No thought is given to the possibility that help could come from anywhere else. Jesus enters a world that does not expect him. And now he comes upon one of these wretched persons. For thirty-eight years he has lain on his mat – as long as the ancient people of God sojourned in the desert. How often he wanted to have tried to enter the waters. On all fours. Crying out, Help me! How often he wanted to be nearer his goal! But again and again disappointment – overrun, shoved aside, cheated out of life.

"Do you want to be made well?" Jesus asks him – or after all the disappointments over thirty-eight years have you capitulated to the unchanging nature of your condition and given up, expecting nothing else? "Sir, I have no one." I have no one who takes the least interest in me or cares about me, for whom I even matter. The lonely individual. How many may there be in our city who would say, "I have no one"? No one among the 230,000. No one who looks once at me, who even once asks me how things are going, who notices that I cannot go on. Perhaps some resonate with the answer of the lonely man: from the people here I expect nothing more and now I expect nothing at all. But perhaps there will come, after all, one who will actually notice me and take an interest in my situation.

And now Jesus comes to this man who has no one, the merciful companion that he needs, without whom he will continue to decline, and for whom he has waited, so far in vain.

My brothers and sisters! This is always true and for everyone: There is one who is the companion of those who are stuck on the side of the road, overlooked by some and shoved aside by others, the brotherly partner who gives himself to them and does not abandon them. None of us needs to say anymore, "I have no one."

And each of us for whom things are going well, as a disciple of Jesus, should open our eyes and our heart in such a way that no longer is there anyone nearby who is overlooked, abandoned, forgotten, or isolated, and should share with him his (Jesus') joy.

II.

Jesus associates with the lonely. He frees him from his miserable paralysis.

Already Jesus' brotherly gift to this person – the breakthrough of the circle of isolation and resignation – is enormous for him. But in Jesus not only has the compassionate brother come to him, but this is also the one who brings life and contentment, the one through whose work God restores creation. In his encounter with Jesus the entire person is made whole. He is free of the paralysis which had limited and diminished him.

The healing takes place due to the word Jesus speaks. This word is not some magical formula nor are they words of exorcism, but rather a command to the sick person: "Stand up, take your mat and walk." Stand up and walk – as if he could do that! As if he had that kind of strength! That is precisely what he cannot do. This command assumes that he is already healed. That is, in fact, the case with all imperatives in the Bible (Follow me! Love your enemies! Be not afraid!): They all command something that no one, using one's own innate ability can do. It goes beyond one's own strength. All those commands which are new to human beings and the world can only be complied with in faith in the one who commands – and in the assurance that he is able to do what he commands. In this order there is planted a quite wonderful expectation: "Stand up, take your mat and walk." That is the challenge, to do something that goes against thirty-eight years of experience, to forget the frustrations of half a lifetime. But that is what one might cry out to a long-standing alcoholic: Stop it, take your bottle and throw it away. – Or to a husband who is seeing another woman: Enough already! Don't go there anymore. Throw away the key to her house. – Or to someone who is committed to informing on persons in his circle of friends: Not another word! Tell your employers that they will hear nothing more from you. Will they not answer, "I have so often tried that. It doesn't work. I can't do it"?

The lame man could not do it either if he depended on his own strength and on all the vain efforts in his life so far. But the command to stand up did not come from just anyone, but from the physician beyond compare, from the restorer of the world. Whoever unconditionally entrusts himself or herself to him and obeys without hesitation, qualification, or objection is made whole, begins to live, and has become part of the new creation. Indeed, this miracle of the new, healthy life happens only to those who are completely obedient: to those who carry away the old mattress and do not save it just in case it is needed again – because one never knows; who do not simply lock the mat up in a closet, but throws it away; who reduce their degree of adultery, but break it off altogether; who not only make harmless reports to their dark employers, but say nothing more at all. There are thousands who obey only half-heartedly and want to hold open the possibility of returning to the old life and end up getting nothing out of life. And there are thousands who from experience can say, " He sets the prisoner free."[40]

### III.

Jesus associates with the lonely. He frees him from his miserable paralysis. He makes him the unmistakable sign of the dawn of the salvific future.

If the command to stand up for a man who has been paralyzed for such a long time is an incredible challenge to his faith, then so is the command to carry his mat into the city an even bigger one because it was the sabbath. The prophet Jeremiah says it expressly:

---

[40] Translator's note: This quote is the title of a book by Paul Humburg, Die hart gebundenen macht er frei, published in 1959 by Neukirchener Verlag. The title is based on Psalm 146:7 from which the English translation is taken.

"For the sake of your lives, take care that you do not bear a burden on the sabbath day or bring it in by the gates of Jerusalem" (17:21). The command therefore contains the challenge to act against God's clear decree. In obeying Jesus' directive, the crippled man expresses his certainty that the one who is standing before me can require nothing of me that goes against God. That is quite impossible.

But what are we to make of this unnecessary, superfluous, deliberately provocative command of Jesus to pointedly break the sabbath? The command did not have to include carrying his mat! Surely that could have waited another day. Was Jesus simply being a foolish provocateur? No. This man who had been made well was supposed to parade openly on the streets of the holy city on the sabbath with his now expendable mat. Now we see that to which the sabbath points, namely, the healing of creation. God wants to take joy again in the creation as on the first sabbath: "Behold, it is all good." Now is the time to which the sabbath points, now is the time of fulfillment. This is a time of insisting on the ancient commandment against disobeying God, against rejecting and disputing what God is at work doing in Jesus Christ, at work renewing the creation step by step, heart by heart, so that the great festival can be celebrated, a celebration without end, in which all may participate.

From this we must also hear the admonition to the healed one: "See, you have been made well! Do not sin any more, so that nothing worse happens to you." You have become a partner in the time of salvation, you have come into contact with Jesus and have received from him new life, you are part of the new creation. Do not disavow your new reality! Never let the living contact with Jesus be broken! Do not relapse into your past, into the old, bleak life. Otherwise, you would not only have to live hopelessly for thirty-eight years, but forever. To have encountered Jesus and to have been given life by him and then to leave that life for something else – that is worse than never to have met him.

Dear brothers and sisters, Jesus has sought us out in our misery. None of us can say any longer that they have no one who comes and stays with them. Jesus Christ has freed us for a full, undiminished life. He wants us to stay with him and cling to him and to be his eyes looking for the overlooked, the forgotten, the afflicted. And as a sign of, and witness to, the salvation that has dawned in him we are to point to, tell of, and live out something of the joyful celebration of the new creation. Amen.

# John 8:12-14
## December 26, 1987
### Second Day of Christmas in Schneeberg in the Ore Mountains

Again Jesus spoke to them, saying, "I am the light of the world. Whoever follows me will never walk in darkness but will have the light of life." Then the Pharisees said to him, "You are testifying on your own behalf; your testimony is not valid." Jesus answered, "Even if I testify on my own behalf, my testimony is valid because I know where I have come from and where I am going, but you do not know where I am from or where I am going."

Dear Friends, "I am the light of the world," Jesus says about himself. When he said that, he most definitely did not have in mind a burning candle on the Christmas tree. Nor only because there was nothing of the sort at that time, but also because it would be something for thoughtful reflection – as an escape from the hard reality of our life. When Jesus said about himself, "I am the light of the world," his thought was more likely on the sun. It is not, like the candle, a nice addition to life, but rather the condition of life. Where I am, Jesus says, it is neither simply as a bit of coziness nor where one can dream and reflect for awhile (as nice as that may be), but rather where I am, it is as clear as day, where life can flourish in the hard reality of this world, where the darkness of death must give way and the terror of night must flee.

Jesus is making an enormous claim in this self-designation. He is not only saying, I am a light in this world – one among others –, but "I am the light of the world," the one with which no other can compare and which no other can replace – not the light of science because even this light cannot be directed toward the darkness of death or the fiercest darkness of this world or some deadly madness. We want to see ourselves as powerful, we can take life into our own hands, we need only ourselves, no one else. Against this deadly gloom with which human beings have empowered themselves and which kills them, only I am able to contend, says Jesus. "I am the light of the world."

It is no wonder that Jesus meets with immediate objections. "You are testifying on your own behalf; your testimony is not valid." You are a witness in your own cause, you are claiming something for yourself – and that doesn't count for anything with us. But we know who you are. You are the son of Joseph and Mary. Your parents are honorable people and you have learned an honest trade. What we have seen and heard of you is something indeed. We do not dispute that, but "the light of the world"? That is too much. Later they will ask him, "Who do you think you are?"

Perhaps today it would sound something like this: We have seen too many persons who passed themselves off as being lights and who claimed that a new era began with them, a new shining day in human history. And then these supposed lights turn out to be will-o-the-wisps or even evil gangs. We do not argue that Jesus was a very special person, one who meant really well with others, but "the light of the world"? That would mean that life depends on him. One should not make such a claim about oneself. There would have to be witnesses who experienced that and could credibly confirm it. At least one.

I know one – no, I don't know him, but I know of one who confirmed that. An un-Christmas-like witness from a very un-Christmas-like situation.

It was in the Buchenwald concentration camp. A man stood in the roll call square, completely alone among the thousands in the camp, at the end of his rope and without faith, fully determined to walk at night into the electric fence and bring to an end this wretched existence. Then in this place of terror and doubt he heard a loud, clear voice ring out above the camp of 20,000 prisoners. This voice cried out from the barred window of a bunker cell: "Jesus Christ says, I am the light of the world; whoever follows me will never walk in darkness but will have the light of life." That was the voice of the Rhineland pastor, Paul Schneider, who had been imprisoned there in a dark cell for thirteen months until under brutal mistreatment by his guards he died. The one who told the story added, "He saved me by his loud cry. From that point on I knew that there was someone with me."

What Jesus says here about himself proved to be true in the life of a human being. In a desperate situation in which death seemed to be the only way out. In this exceedingly dark night this light that Jesus is and that he provides shone so brightly that a man again received courage to live. This word of Jesus about himself is reflected and confirmed in the preserved human life which would have been extinguished in the darkness without this word.

Indeed, a witness for the truth of this claim by Jesus would be only slightly credible, especially in such an extreme situation. But I think that in this Christmas worship service there are other witnesses who could confirm this from their own experience and from more normal life situations. Yes, it's true what Jesus says. He brought light when my life filled with darkness, when I no longer knew if I could go on, when we were finished with each other, when we were stubborn or had felt trapped and we saw no way out. I think there may be some among us whose own experience is captured in Paul Gerhardt's hymn: "When I faced the dark night of the soul, you were my sun; the sun that brought me light, life, joy, and bliss."[41] Or words by Johannes Scheffler: "I thank you, true sun, that you brought me the splendor of your light. I thank you, bliss of heaven, that you have made me happy and free."[42] I think there may be some among us for whom these words are not merely lyrics or nice poetry, but experienced reality of their life, even if they would naturally say it differently.

To be sure, such testimonies cannot prove that Jesus is right in claiming to be the light of the world. Others cannot claim that for him. Only he can legitimately make that claim for himself: "Even if I testify on my own behalf, my testimony is valid because I know where I have come from." We cannot prove it, but we can point to him through our experiences. Perhaps some could tell how he helped them in their seemingly dull marriage, to see the other with fresh eyes and to discover what they have in each other. Or others can tell how Jesus liberated them from alcohol when they could not escape it from destroying their life, and how light came again into their joyless existence. Or others still can tell how he suddenly

---

[41] Translator's note: This is my translation of the third stanza of Gerhardt's hymn, "Ich stehe an deiner Krippen hier".
[42] Translator's note: This is my translation of the fifth stanza of Scheffler's hymn, "Ich will dich lieben, meine Stärke".

brought light into their confusion and pointed them in a navigable direction, and how he comforted them in their unfathomable depression.

"I am the light of the world." When Jesus said that, perhaps he not only had the sun in mind, but something else as well. The majesty of the light that God provides which conforms to God's existence is not created as the sun is. Psalm 104:2 says, "wrapped in light as with a garment" and in I Timothy we read, "God dwells in unapproachable light" (6:16). And now in him, the son of Mary, this unapproachable light has come to us and has become accessible to us. "Light from Light, born from God", "Light from uncreated Light."[43]

Here it is. In the poor infant Jesus, born in a stable. In a human being. In this human being. "The light shines in the darkness," as is written in today's Gospel lesson. It shines, "And the darkness did not overcome it" (John 1:5). Thus, even the despairing darkness of this world persists, blocks out this light, and thinks it is better off with its own lights. It itself is so enlightened, so clairvoyant, that it needs no light other than its own. And yet, this divine light that is made real in Jesus persists. The darkness has not grasped it, but it has also not been able to extinguish it. "There shines a light in the middle of the night and makes us all children of the light."[44] Whoever lives in this light, whoever submits to it, is a participant in him who is light. As Jesus says here, "Whoever follows me will never walk in darkness but will have the light of life."

Christmas is not simply a time to light candles for a few days and sing some of our favorite hymns ("O Jesus, Beautiful Christmas Sun"[45]) – surely we can and should do that too – but, above all, Christmas invites us to deal with Jesus, to be near him, to confide in him, to walk along his path because in walking together he opens up to us as the light that disperses the darkness. Only so can we have lively experiences and know what life with him is like.

---

[43] Translator's note: "Uncreated light" – In the Eastern Orthodox tradition this is the light on the Mount of Transfiguration.
[44] Translator's note: This is my translation of the 4th stanza of Martin Luther's hymn "Gelobet seiest du, Jesu Christ".
[45] Translator's note: These words open stanza 5 of Kaspar Friedrich Nachtenhöfer's hymn "Dies ist die Nacht". It is my translation.

Whoever follows Jesus becomes aware that the life of Jesus, and therefore life with Jesus, has a Christmas characteristic, namely, a marked downward trajectory towards earth. "He came to earth poor, so that He might have sympathy for us."[46] – "Though he was rich, yet for your sakes he became poor" (II Cor. 8:9). Whoever is upwardly ambitious still lives in darkness and death. Children of light follow the movement of Jesus – not seeking to move upward, but rather into the depths, to those whom others will not have, who live difficult lives, those left behind by society, those left in the lurch, the overlooked, the passed by, the excluded, those of poor character, the unloved. Whoever sets out in that direction and offers a bit of his or her life, whoever consumes a few millimeters of his or her candle, so to speak, that person's experience is not one of a diminution of life, but rather one of an expansion of life.

"Whoever follows me," Jesus says – whoever is prepared, as I am, to be with those who are poor in love, poor in joy, poor in faith and in hope, who hunger for human contact, for one who sees them, who will listen to them, who will offer their hands, who will pray with them – whoever is prepared for that, as Jesus is, will not live a poor life, but will, in fact, begin to live for the first time. "Whoever follows me," Jesus says, whoever does as I do, "will have the light of life." Perhaps it occurs to someone now – now or on your way home – to whom you would have to go if you want to follow the Christmas movement of Jesus – not in the heights, but in the depths – and thereby experience life. True life experiences are found in the depths.

One more thing: Whoever depends on Jesus, whoever follows him discovers that Jesus, in fact, is the light for the world – that not only that person, and not only the church, but also that the world is loved by God, that God is there the night before Christ was born, to establish the kingdom in the confused world event, the kingdom in which righteousness and peace kiss passionately, so that the powers of death do not have the last word. "The darkness is passing away and the true light is already shining," writes John (I John 2:8).

---

[46] Translator's note: From Bach's Christmas Cantata for the First Day of Christmas.

Whoever stays on the path of Jesus discovers some astounding things today: As Jesus' words all at once begin to shine so brightly, they even become intelligible to politicians. To cite only one example: "Blessed are the meek, for they will inherit the earth" (the earth-kingdom), Jesus says in the Sermon on the Mount (Mt. 5:5). Thus, the earth belongs to those who renounce force. Indeed, the earth will belong to persons only when they stop threatening others with weapons, when they remove images of enemies which they used to build up their arms. Today not only churches and peace groups are saying that, but reasonable politicians are as well. That comes from Jesus who is not only the light for the church, but also for the world. By means of his enlightening and manifest word he guards the world against decline into chaotic darkness.

Whoever stays on the path of Jesus knows that Jesus is not a small light for one's personal life, but that person discovers, astonishingly, that Jesus is the light that confronts the powers of darkness in the world, "dispels with glorious splendor the darkness everywhere."[47] It cannot prevail against this light, and its dark tricks are brought to light and can no longer spread unhindered. "Whoever follows me," Jesus says, "will never walk in darkness but will have the light of life." If we cling to him, we will not grope in the darkness in view of world events. We will see the world as it is. We do not need to glorify it, but neither do we need to demonize it. We can look at the world in light of the hope of Jesus Christ and remain on guard against fatalistic resignation which does not expect anything and only declares, Nothing makes any sense. Because of Christmas Eve, stand firm: The world will not remain as it is. That one who was born Christmas night said, "See, I am making all things new" (Rev. 21:5).

Dear brothers and sisters, we are invited to hold on to Jesus, to stay in his light so that we can live as children of light. Jesus, the light for the world, has said to those who have become his own, "You are the light of the world" (Mt. 5:14). Whoever you are – as a congregation or as individuals – there the world is a bit brighter, friendlier, warmer, there people are refreshed, there some find meaning again and life is no longer bleak.

---

[47] Stanza 3 in "Lo, How a Rose e'er Blooming" in the Evangelical Lutheran hymnal, Worship (German: "Es ist ein Ros' entsprungen").

Dear friends, if we are with him, living in his light, no darkness can be so dark that we have to succumb to it, no situation so desperate or untenable that we would prefer to die, no depression so deep that tears of hopelessness are all that remain. Instead, he will be there with his loving devotion, his deep comfort, his clear signpost, his final illumination of purpose. What did the man in the concentration camp say when the darkness had become so dark that he wanted to throw away his life? "He saved me by his loud cry. From that point on I knew that there was someone with me."

Those that know that someone is with them know that the darkness must retreat over and over again. They have enough light in which to live and in which to die. Amen.

# John 21:1-14
## April 10, 1983
Sunday after Easter in the Protestant Health Care Facility in Neinstedt near Quedlinburg

After these things Jesus showed himself again to the disciples by the Sea of Tiberias; and he showed himself in this way. Gathered there together were Simon Peter, Thomas called the Twin, Nathanael of Cana in Galilee, the sons of Zebedee, and two others of his disciples. Simon Peter said to them, "I am going fishing." They said to him, "We will go with you." They went out and got into the boat, but that night they caught nothing.

Just after daybreak, Jesus stood on the beach; but the disciples did not know that it was Jesus. Jesus said to them, "Children, you have no fish, have you?" They answered, "No." He said to them, "Cast the net to the right side of the boat, and you will find some." So they cast it, and now they were not able to haul it in because there were so many fish. That disciple whom Jesus loved said to Peter, "It is the Lord!" When Simon Peter heard that it was the Lord, he put on some clothes, for he was naked, and jumped into the sea. But the other disciples came in the boat, dragging the net full of fish, for they were not far from the land, only about a hundred yards off.

When they had gone ashore, they saw a charcoal fire there, with fish on it and bread. Jesus said to them, "Bring some of the fish that you have just caught." So Simon Peter went aboard and hauled the net ashore, full of large fish, a hundred fifty-three of them; and though there were so many, the net was not torn. Jesus said to them, "Come and have breakfast." Now none of the disciples dared to ask him, "Who are you?" because they knew it was the Lord. Jesus came and took the bread and gave it to them, and did the same with the fish. This was now the third time that Jesus appeared to the disciples after he was raised from the dead.

Dear Friends! This enigmatic Easter story, which takes place at dawn with a veil of mist resting over the lake and gradually lifting in the morning light, opens with a sense of failure on the part of Jesus' disciples. One of these seven quite young men could no longer sit around in this crippling atmosphere after Good Friday in which nothing was happening, in which all were despondent, and in which no one knew what was going to happen next. Easter did not yet seem real to them, even though the risen Christ had already appeared to them.

In any case, one of the disciples was no longer willing to simply let things continue without doing something. His view now was that they had to find something to do. "I am going fishing," says Peter. When one person breaks the silence and becomes active, he can always count on others to follow suit. "Then we will go with you." – "We are coming too," the other six say, happy not having to sit around day-dreaming. And so they climb into a boat, cast out, and get to work.

Why didn't they catch anything on this night? Why did this common effort go so awry? It seems clear to me that here the evangelist does not simply want to tell a fish story which Peter, the fisherman, instigated with his colleagues. Rather, what is being told here is transparently a missionary action which the disciple, Peter, starts with his brothers. Why didn't they catch anything this night? Why did they return empty-handed? Because it was an action they took on their own, an action without Jesus. Because they had forgotten what the Lord had said to them, "Apart from me you can do nothing" (John 15:5b).

The evangelist wants to say to a community that has been active and stirred up: After Easter and in spite of Easter church people can believe as if nothing at all had changed. People can do as Peter and the other disciples do here and, in spite of the resurrection of the Lord having already occurred and in spite of their earlier experiences, live in such a way as if nothing has happened, as if they are left to fend for themselves, as if they now finally need to take their own initiative and do something. In fact, that is not only the case here, but it is the constant temptation in the church, namely, to go about its work in a high-handed way, to go about stubbornly working on anything because there is no sign or trace of the risen Lord.

And now the community of disciples, the church of the risen Lord, and we can learn something: The church achieves nothing, produces nothing, brings nothing in if she depends on herself, if she undertakes something out of unbelief or impatience, even if the initiator of such an undertaking is such a respectable man as Peter who actually understands something about fishing. "That night they caught nothing."

Well, if after such a high-handed action the community of disciples at least acknowledge, in response to the Lord's question, that they had caught nothing, they are also saying that he counts for nothing. If they do not already count as success the mere fact that something was done, at least they had actually been up and about doing something.

The evangelist tells us that the risen Lord stood unrecognized on the shore as this action group returned disappointed from their vain venture, and he asked them, "Children, you have no fish, have you?" Nothing caught? The Lord asks them very precisely about the results of their efforts on which they had so arrogantly set out because they had not reckoned with being with him anymore. He does not ask them whether they have had a good outing or whether they have seen any fish, but whether they had caught any fish. And even this they have to deny. If they are asked about their catch, which was the only point of their outing, they are unable to answer: We have caught nothing, but there was a lot going on out there and we had good conversations among ourselves. It was well worth it.

When the Lord asks his disciples about the fruit of their mission, they are unable to answer: No one was converted, but the organization was perfect, the collection was good, and the public impression was considerable. It would have been all right if the group of disciples had had the courage not to misrepresent their empty results as a success or to attribute their failed efforts to adverse circumstances – the headwind or the noise from the other boats. Their failed actions will have the best results for the disciples if the next time they learn to count on their Lord and wait for his instructions.

And he does not leave his people without instructions: "Cast the net to the right side of the boat, and you will find some." Now it is no longer Peter but Jesus who springs into action with his command and his promise. They should cast their nets on the right side as designated by him, on the side where he has laid his hand and will bless it. It is not left to the inclination of the disciples as to where they should be working. Peter and his friends do not ask what sense it makes to cast their nets on the other side, and they also do not ask whether they really need to do it immediately. Instead, they move from one side to the other, as the Lord instructed. That is what is crucial when we in a congregation or in the larger church plan our missionary work, namely, that we let our Lord point to the place where we need to be active, the persons to whom we should turn, with whom we should be in conversation in order to bring them into conversation with him, that we stop thinking something is going on when everything is going on.

Whenever the disciples follow the bidding of their Lord and trust his promise, whenever they listen to his directions, the nets will not be empty and indeed will be full. "So they cast it, and now they were not able to haul it in because there were so many fish." In view of this development one of the participants cried out this confession: "It is the Lord!" Only one person could do this. By his word an empty net was filled to the breaking point. Only one person could do this. For people for whom courage had sunk from futile action to nothing at all, the heart is full to overflowing. "It is the Lord!" He has power over creation, he has power over hearts.

The outcome of the catch demonstrates to disciples of all times what the Lord wants from them – people are to be won for Jesus, a people are to be brought together for the Lord. For the Lord! The church is catching nothing in its nets. That distinguishes it from all other organizations in today's world that are attracting people. They want to keep the people for themselves. Thus, people live in such a fear of being taken, even for ransom. And such fear is justified! The disciples don't want to win people for themselves. Rather, they want to bring them together for their good fortune. It's not an end for someone who is caught, but that person's happiness. A person does not lose his or her life, but gains it. (In any case, I have not yet known anyone who has been won for Jesus who feels as if they had been taken for ransom.) Here one does not become part of the prey of captured persons, nor a godly person, but rather one belongs to the Lord in whom one becomes free.

Whoever has been caught here, whoever has been seized is not someone caught in the clutches of a predator or tangled in the ropes of a fisherman, but has been rescued by the Lord. It is a matter of being caught, but being caught by him. We cast our nets, but he is the one who drives the fish into the net. Because it is he, we do not need either to employ pressure tactics or all kinds of sophisticated baits – with blues and beer – to lure people into the nets. We may leave it to him to bring them in. The catch belongs to him, not to us.

The Lord also lets his disciples see the result – 153 large fish. Ancient zoologists knew of 153 kinds of fish. The number tells us that everything that was generally to be caught among fish was in this net which the disciples had cast on their Lord's command. So, when it comes to human beings, everything will be gathered into one people that belong to the Lord. Out of all peoples the church, the new humanity, will be the result of nets cast by Jesus' disciples.

The Lord intended it for the world because he loves it. He wants everyone, both near and far. And this catch is held together by a net that has room for such a variety, and yet it is so strong that such a quantity cannot tear it. This breadth and this strength must be there if it is to be reflected in the church. The church must be so broad that not only persons from all nations have a place in it, but persons of the widest variety of character, lifestyles, and backgrounds also have a place. Our church is so tightly-woven that only a few small pious fish have a place in it. It must be wider! But not so wide that it is no longer clear that those in the net really are claimed by the Lord of the catch, that they belong to him, that the net has no institutional leaks. Wherever the openness becomes programmatic, the church becomes a playground, a gathering with all kinds of attractive, but non-binding offers. And wherever the steadiness is elevated to a program, the circle closes in on itself, a closed assembly, an elite group of the elect takes place. The openness and the strength of the church are, at bottom, the mystery of Jesus Christ who binds us to him and thereby grants us freedom.

It is the Lord who fills the broad and strong net, but it is the disciples who cast the net on Jesus' command. The Lord wants us there to fish. With Jesus one is always active. "So they cast the net," "then they hauled the net full of fish," was the disciples' experience. They had more than they could handle.

What does that look like in practical terms? First of all, everyone participates in this fishing experience. The Lord did not make his disciples anglers, but fishermen. They are not to work as individuals but together, as a community of disciples, as a church. But what does casting nets look like, practically? How does it happen? It happens when we as a community of disciples bring persons together in every possible way with the gospel, when we engage them in conversation, bringing Jesus into the conversation, and allowing Jesus' love surface.

On Easter Monday in the cathedral hall in Magdeburg a young man was baptized. He shared how he had come into contact with Jesus Christ. A few years ago he, who had never darkened the door of a church, was on vacation and he attended a worship service in a village church. Only once. There were only a few older women there, but they had welcomed him in such a friendly way. That made an impression on him. A year later, again on vacation, he had the same experience in another village church. Then an acquaintance gave him a book "about religion," as he put it. And there it began. He attended worship more and more often until it became clear to him that he had to be baptized.

Before Easter I had a conversation with two young couples with children about baptism. One of the mothers remarked that she had been baptized as an adult. When I asked how she had come to Christ, she said that her fiance had given her the children's book, **Das Wort Läuft**.[48] As she read it, something touched her heart, and so it has continued. Casting the net can look as simple as handing a book to another: Read it! How many have come into contact with Jesus Christ in this way, that someone has taken it as preparation for student ministry? In Magdeburg I have gotten to know young people who have taken their vacation to go on the street to share the gospel and to speak to youth, inviting them to have a conversation. There were no seminary students. Casting nets happens in a variety of ways. The purpose is always to bring

---

[48] Translator's note: In English The Word Runs. In German it's a biblical reader for children. Published in 1973 by Evangelische Verlaganstalt.

persons into contact with Jesus, to draw them into the realm of his radiance and the force field of his love.

The disciples experience the sending-out-Lord as the simultaneously self-giving Lord. Those whom he sends into the world he also invites to his table. "When they had gone ashore, they saw a charcoal fire there, with fish on it, and bread.... Jesus said to them, 'Come and have breakfast!... Jesus came and took the bread and gave it to them, and did the same with the fish."

It is noteworthy that the disciples caught the fish. But before they reach land, there are fish already on the fire which the Lord gives them. That means that the disciples – and therefore we – do not need to live by our own efforts. Long before whatever our work may produce, the Lord has prepared what we need. We may come forward and take from his hand. All is prepared.

Those whom the Lord invites to his table, into his community, he gives the assurance of his full, real presence. "None of the disciples dared to ask him, 'Who are you?' because they knew it was the Lord." At the Lord's table problems cease. His presence is no longer problematic and no longer needs to be an issue. Whoever goes and receives the bread, to them the Lord gives himself. No longer can anyone question that it is the Lord, the Lord who loves them. Even if their faith is, again and again, as weak as that of these seven disciples. Amen.

# Acts 3:1-10
## August 29, 1982
### 12th Sunday after Trinity Sunday, in St. Jacob's Church in Schönebeck/Elbe

One day Peter and John were going up to the temple at the hour of prayer, at three o'clock in the afternoon. And a man lame from birth was being carried in. People would lay him daily at the gate of the temple called the Beautiful Gate so that he could ask for alms from those entering the temple. When he saw Peter and John about to go into the temple, he asked them for alms. Peter looked intently at him, as did John, and said, "Look at us." And he fixed his attention on them, expecting to receive something from them. But Peter said, "I have no silver or gold, but what I have I give you; in the name of Jesus Christ of Nazareth, stand up and walk." And he took him by the right hand and raised him up; and immediately his feet and ankles were made strong. Jumping up, he stood and began to walk, and he entered the temple with them, walking and leaping and praising God. All the people saw him walking and praising God, and they recognized him as the one who used to sit and ask for alms at the Beautiful Gate of the temple; and they were filled with wonder and amazement at what had happened to him.

Dear Friends, It is fortuitous that, on this Sunday when the Schniewindhaus[49] celebrates its 25th anniversary as a home for spiritual and physical renewal of our church province, the text for today's sermon is this account of the healing of the lame man. Indeed, this report tells of the strength of the name of Jesus Christ. From the very beginning one of the chief characteristics of the Schniewindhaus is that the power of the name of Jesus is to be trusted. And with this name in these 25 years wonderful things have been experienced, and as a result a stream of blessings have

---

[49] Translator's note: This "house" is a community that serves as a retreat center. Although founded in the early 20th century, in 1957 it came under the auspices of the Protestant Church and began to address spiritual matters.

flowed into our church. In this worship service there are undoubtedly persons who could tell of such experiences. That will surely happen sometime today, and that is as it should be.

However, because God's word is always more than our experiences, because it makes possible those experiences in the first place and enables them to be rightly understood, we do not now tell of our experiences, but rather preach on this passage from Acts and, furthermore, say what we have heard from this story as the word the Lord wants to say today to this congregation.

To summarize briefly: To act in the strength of the name of Jesus means:

1. To look at people in their misery.

2. To help people out of their misery.

I.

The lame beggar at the door of the temple had come to terms with his situation. At 40 he was an old man. He was never able to stand on his own legs. Who knows how many years his relatives had carried him, day after day, to the temple portal and then brought him home again in the evening. Here was one who was unable to feel fully human. To be constantly dependent on other people for help – be it from his own parents or siblings – is, over time, humiliating.

But that was not everything. He was allowed to sit in front of the temple, but not to enter it. There was no place inside for crippled persons or other persons with disabilities. There was something in their lives that did not sit right with God. This man was, literally, "The Man Outside."[50] And worst of all, this lame man never counted on the possibility that in his life anything could fundamentally change. Even his soul had become crippled. He no longer expected anything from other persons than a few coins for subsistence. Crouched on the ground, he had become used to

---

[50] Translator's note: "Draussen vor der Tür" is the German and is the title of a play by Wolfgang Borchert (1947).

passers-by either ignoring him or treating him like a hollow shell into which they might toss a couple of pennies. Nothing offended him anymore. It no longer mattered at all to him whether anyone gave him anything or not. He had not yet had anyone take him seriously as a human being, and, in all likelihood, he would never see that happen. For his relatives themselves who deposited him daily at his customary place in front of the temple, it was only important that he be picked up at the end of the day. A miserable existence.

The story goes that Rainer Maria Rilke[51] had to pass by daily an old woman beggar. Inwardly, she was so crippled and empty that she no longer looked up when someone tossed a coin into her apron. Rilke said to his young woman companion, "We should give her more." His companion took a larger coin out of her purse. "Not that," Rilke objected. The next day Rilke laid a rose in the beggar's lap. She looked up at him astonished, stood up, and for a week was nowhere to be seen. Then she came and sat again where she had sat earlier. Rilke's companion asked, "On what was she able to live?" Rilke replied, "On the rose." With that she was revived and had lived a week long because someone had honored her as a full human being, as a person who lived not on pennies and not even on larger amounts of money, but on love, on being seen as a full human being.

How was Rilke able to do that? I think it was because such stories took place as the one told here by Luke. And this story could only happen, in turn, because Peter and John had experienced it with Jesus. Wherever he encountered persons in misery or when they were brought to him, he never ignored human pain, but always stopped what he was doing. He did not look away as if they had nothing to do with him. Instead, he looked at them in the eye with compassion. He stopped and had time for them. He never passed by someone who needed him. He never said, "I have something more important to do." Never did he say, "I am simply too tired right now." He was there to help the person become an unhampered, fully human person, and thereby be able to live as a beloved child of God. How often does it happen in the Gospels

---

[51] Rilke (1875-1926), a poet and novelist, was born in Prague and died in Montreux, Switzerland. He wrote in the German language.

that when Jesus caught sight of someone in pain, "he looked at him and had pity on him," his heart melted within him.

And so it also is here. The two apostles do not walk past the beggar. It was time for worship and they had to be careful not to enter the temple too late. This is what is reported: "Peter looked intently at him, as did John, and said, 'Look at us.' And he fixed his attention on them, expecting to receive something from them." What a sight for sore eyes!

In them was being prepared the turning-point and the end of the beggar's misery. For once, not to be ignored, but to be acknowledged! And the eyes that looked back at him and into which he looked were eyes opened by Jesus. Those eyes saw the complete distress of the person whose visible exterior hid what lay behind it. We have busied ourselves keeping the invisible pain of human beings out of sight. We want to see as little of it as possible.

Beggars don't really appear here much. A man like the one in this story would be taken to a home and cared for there. We have managed to keep the pain of the elderly and the sick out of sight. That's why we have nursing homes and hospitals. And that's a good thing. But it would be a grave error to think that human misery has somehow become less acute. It is a thousand times worse than we think: the pain of the person who believes he is not important, who suspects he would not be missed if he were no longer around, and who has concluded that nothing will change. The distress of the person who is unable to grasp the thought that he is loved, that he is a child of God and thus is fully and completely human.

To act in the name of Jesus means, above all, to notice this person's pain, to see it. It means not to hide from it, and not to turn away from it. On the contrary, it means to confront it.

II.

The two men on their way to worship confront it out of their association with Jesus. When they saw the crippled beggar, the question may have occurred to them, Shall we leave this man sitting before the temple in his misery while we go inside and praise and glorify the God of Israel, the Father of Jesus Christ? The answer could only be, No. That would be wrong. We would be like the priest and the Levite about whom Jesus told, who passed by the beaten man in order to carry out their religious duties. That's why the two paused and looked at him. They looked him in the eyes and invited him to look at them. Of course, they did not have what he expected from them, the one thing that could possibly help him. "I have no silver or gold," Peter tells him. Some kind of pious aphorism? Only a few sympathetic words? I can imagine that the crippled man thought, Please no! I have enough of that!

No, they do not come simply offering empty talk. Nor do they simply offer a rose (although it could mean a lot, enabling a person to live eight days!). No, much more, they offer the empowered, compassionate command of the risen one: "'In the name of Jesus Christ of Nazareth, stand up and walk! And he took him by the right hand and raised him up." An incantation? A magical formula? No, a word spoken in faith in Jesus' authority and bringing with it faith in Jesus' authority. It all happened in a second. The command to stand issued in the name of Jesus Christ is spoken, the hand of the beggar grasped. He is no longer sitting down, taking the challenge as a futile one, but obeying the command, with this word he gripped the outstretched hand and, standing up, he experiences that he has been helped.

What happens here cannot be analyzed psychologically. It is the miracle of faith in Jesus and through Jesus. Stammering, Peter can only say to those who see the crippled man leaping throughout the temple what has taken place here: "By faith in his (Jesus') name, his name itself has made this man strong, whom you see and know; and the faith that is through Jesus has given him this perfect health in the presence of all of you" (3:16). The word spoken in the name of Jesus reached his ears and heart, but it literally penetrated his bones. It brought him to his knees.

Not only did he receive healthy bones and no longer lives with the pain of his illness, but all of his misery is gone. He has been made whole and has been restored to being a full human being. That is made evident in that he did not run home, but went into the temple with the two disciples of Jesus and there he jumped for joy, praising God. Whoever praises God is undiminished and is a fully and complete human being. Here not only did something internal take place – a change of heart –, but something observable, a transformation which springs before others' eyes: "All the people saw him walking and praising God.... And they were filled with wonder and amazement at what had happened to him."

Dear brothers and sisters! Like Peter and John, we belong to the community of the crucified and risen Christ, to his church. It is no different for us than for them: "We do not have gold or silver." We cannot promise to eliminate all the pain in the whole world. The two apostles did not say unsympathetically, "Unfortunately, we don't have anything." Obviously, they did not see that as a disadvantage. They had no inferiority complex such that they could not compete here. They did come across as being without resources. "But what we have...," they say. What do they have and what do we have? Like them, we have the name Jesus Christ. Do we trust this name as much as they did? I have never dared someone in a wheelchair to say, "In the name of Jesus Christ, stand up!" Is it because I do not expect anything from the name Jesus Christ? Is the fact that among us – in the community of Jesus Christ – there are persons with serious bodily disabilities an indication that either as healthy persons we or they do not expect anything, or at least not much, from the name of Jesus? Then the message of the power of Jesus would not be a joyful one, but a painful, even a deadly, message. I know of persons who have been healed through prayer in the name of Jesus or the laying on of hands in the name of Jesus, such that even physicians had no explanation for it and spoke of it as a miracle.

Pastor Jansa, the first leader of the Schniewindhaus, told me that especially at the celebration of Holy Communion, where Jesus is present with his body and blood in the bread and wine, healings took place. I attribute all those things to the name of Jesus. But the name of Jesus is not there for our use. If it were asserted and then no healing took place, it would be a sign of a lack of confidence in the name of Jesus, and the sick would become sicker and the healthy would become sick.

We have the name of Jesus with its power, and therefore we have something that the world does not have. I have witnessed persons who no longer wanted to live, who were at the end of their rope, take courage to continue living under the exhortation of this name, as they literally got back on their feet and thanked God. I knew a woman who was confined to a wheelchair for 40 years and was able to sing, "For joy my heart is ringing; all sorrow disappears; and full of mirth and singing, it wipes away all my tears. The sun that cheers my spirit is Jesus Christ, my king; the heav'n I shall inherit makes me rejoice and sing."[52] The heart can leap for joy even on crutches or in a wheelchair.

"We have no gold or silver." But we have the name of Jesus Christ, the crucified and risen one. I know many people who by the power of the name of Jesus became sensitive to the pain of others – for that of individuals nearby and for the collective pain of persons in the Third World who in the strength of Jesus' name do not turn away from this misery, but endure it and "attack" (in the double meaning of that word[53]) it in its thousand forms, so that people can live unhampered and undiminished lives and as persons loved by God. That happens in the Schniewindhaus, and it happens elsewhere in the church of Jesus Christ.

Often my morning prayer is: "Lord, bless everything that people do today in your name." And it makes me happy to think about all that that entails.

We don't have gold and silver, but we have much more. We have the name of Jesus, the name that is above all names. With this name we become aware of the human pain around us, and in this name people can rise from their misery and rejoice in their humanity and praise God. Amen.

---

[52] Translator's note: This is stanza 13 in Paul Gerhardt's hymn "Ist Gott für mich" which appears in the Evangelical Lutheran hymnal, Worship under the title "If God my Lord Be for Me" (#788).
[53] Translator's note: The German word here is "angreifen" which can mean "attack" and/or "handle".

# Acts 12:1-17
## September 26, 1982
### 16th Sunday after Trinity Sunday at the Conference of the Federal Synod of the Covenant of Protestant Churches in the GDR in Halle

About that time King Herod laid violent hands upon some who belonged to the church. He had James, the brother of John, killed with the sword. After he saw that it pleased the Jews, he proceeded to arrest Peter also. (This was during the festival of Unleavened Bread.) When he had seized him, he put him prison and handed him over to four squads of soldiers to guard him, intending to bring him out to the people after the Passover. While Peter was kept in prison, the church prayed fervently to God for him.

The very night before Herod was going to bring him out, Peter, bound with two chains, was sleeping between two soldiers, while guards in front of the door were keeping watch over the prison. Suddenly an angel of the Lord appeared and a light shone in the cell. He tapped Peter on the side and woke him, saying, "Get up quickly." And the chains fell off his wrists. The angel said to him, "Fasten your belt and put on your sandals." He did so. Then he said to him, "Wrap your cloak around you and follow me." Peter went out and followed him; he did not realize that what was happening with the angel's help was real; he thought he was seeing a vision. After they had passed the first and the second guard, they came before the iron gate leading into the city. It opened for them of its own accord, and they went outside and walked along a lane, when suddenly the angel left him. Then Peter came to himself and said, "Now I am sure that the Lord has sent his angel and rescued me from the hands of Herod and from all that the Jewish people were expecting."

As soon as he realized this, he went to the house of Mary, the mother of John whose other name was Mark, where many had gathered and were praying. When he knocked at the outer gate, a maid named Rhoda came to answer. On recognizing Peter's voice, she was so overjoyed that, instead of opening the gate, she ran in and announced that Peter was standing at the gate. They said to her, "You are out of your mind!" But she insisted that it was so. They said, "It is his angel." Meanwhile Peter continued knocking; and when they opened the gate, they saw him and were amazed. He motioned to them with his hand to be silent, and described for them how the Lord had brought him out of the prison. And he added, "Tell this to James and to the believers." Then he left and went to another place.

Dear Friends! In the book of Acts Luke wants to report how the gospel is spread. The Lord had charged his people to get on the road with the gospel and to bring it to all people. They were not to remain in some small corner, but to labor with the world as their vision. Not only did he proclaim a mission-minded decade, but he also brought to life a community that was to be mission-minded to the ends of the earth.

Now Luke describes how the community fared, a community that was expected to appeal to a Lord whom it could not visibly display. It is good that we learn this from the book of Acts: From the beginning things did not go smoothly; it was not a victory march. There were setbacks as well as miraculous experiences on the strength of the risen Lord. And in both the gospel was proclaimed. Today's text from Acts would like to say to us, The Lord sees to it that the gospel is proclaimed:

1. through the suffering of his people;

2. through the liberation of his people;

3. through the prayers of his people.

## I.

Perhaps in hearing this story we still have the miraculous rescue of Peter in our ears. But something quite different occurred earlier, and we cannot easily ignore it. We cannot forget it and therefore from the outset we need to be restrained from striking any kind of triumphal tones. "About that time," we read, "King Herod laid violent hands upon some who belonged to the church. He had James, the brother of John, killed with the sword." This can happen too. A few people from the church are seized by the king's security forces and killed. On orders from the highest level they murdered one who belonged to Jesus' innermost circle of disciples, one who had been present when Jesus called back to life the daughter of Jairus, one who was there in that unforgettable moment of transfiguration revealing Jesus' true glory, that one who in answer to Jesus' question as to whether he and his brother could drink the cup that he drank answered without blinking an eye, Of course!

This one they had killed. Obviously, no angel had shown up. The church of the crucified Lord must know that he can also demand even this of his messengers, that they be killed, through brutal mistreatment or through gradual nervous breakdown until they are finished. Why does he expect this of his messengers over and over again? Because through their suffering they bear witness to the fact that the life the gospel has given us is worth more than anything else. We will never relinquish that. Never. Not for any price. No one can ever take that from us. Even if they kill us. The life that he has given us cannot be taken from us by anyone. The joy we have in the gospel remains even when there is no more laughter. What he said is true: "and no one will take your joy from you" (John 16:22).

These have testified to this: Hans and Sophie Scholl, Paul Schneider, Dietrich Bonhoeffer, James von Moltke.[54] If the gospel is so important to people that they give up everything for it, if it helps them, if it is so full of hope that they die without any feelings of hatred, then there must be something to it. Thus, the blood of martyrs has become the seed of the church. All suffering that courageously upholds a Christian believer brings the gospel to the attention of others.

---

[54] All of these persons were involved in the German resistance movement to Hitler in World War II and were executed for their involvement.

## II.

The Lord sees to it that the gospel spreads – through the suffering of his people, through the liberation of his people.

The apostle Paul wrote once from prison that his incarceration was beneficial for the gospel. The gospel spreads when people bear witness to it through their suffering that demonstrates that it is important and essential above all else. Something for which someone is no longer willing to take on cannot be worth much.

But the Lord helps spread the gospel in another way which is evidenced here, as he frees persons from hopeless situations and uses them in ways other than as martyrs.

The case of Peter demonstrates, above all, that the gospel can spread in other ways. The king saw that he won additional points with the populace when he took action against Christians. People who did not cooperate are always somewhat annoying. So, the king had their leading figure imprisoned. And he had it done correctly – with 16 guards. For Peter the situation was hopeless. He was chained to two guards and there was an iron gate. There was nothing at all to be done. Any attempt to free himself would have been utterly foolish.

Then came the night before the public hearing, the outcome of which was all but certain. Naturally, Peter would not be executed because he was a Christian. Herod would have had to have fools for state prosecutors if they had not found statements on the basis of which they could bring charges – insulting his majesty, belonging to an opposition alliance, etc. Peter did not sing, as Paul and Silas did later in prison in Philippi (singing alone is not such a good idea), but, it says, he slept. He slept peacefully in the night before the tense hearing. They let him sleep (there weren't any neon lights yet). When one sleeps so deeply, it is irresistibly infectious, and the two guards fell asleep as well.

Then came God's lightning-like action. It was only a matter of a few minutes. We cannot reconstruct what actually happened. Clearly, Luke was not there and Peter himself says he didn't know whether he was awake or dreaming. Only this much is clear: The one who lay in a cell still chained to two guards suddenly finds himself in the middle of the night standing in a deserted alley near the prison. And he will have rubbed his eyes a few times and perhaps pinched himself in the arm to see whether he is really there. Yes, he was really there. Then he will have tried to remember what actually happened. A light in the jail cell suddenly flashed, and he was released from his chains. Then he sensed a slap, and someone said, "Wake up! Get up! Put your shoes and coat on!" (As he looked around, there was perhaps a military coat which he put on as the guards had escorted him.) Then he had run behind the man who had shaken him from sleep as they rushed by the sleeping guards, the iron prison gate suddenly opened, and then the man who had brought him into this alley where he now stood, had disappeared without a trace. To Peter it was clear that it could only have been an angel, a messenger from God! I have not added anything at all to this. I heard it as an order.

Angels cannot be pinned down. They are there, they fulfill their mission, and then they are gone. Any attempts to identify them is futile. "Are not all angels spirits in the divine service, sent to serve for the sake of those who are to inherit salvation?" as it is written in the Letter to the Hebrews (1:14). By no means is it impossible that the messenger of God who set Peter free was an oppositional officer, one who was sympathetic with Christians. Who knows? We will never find out. With angels our imaginations can run wild. Still, in Hebrews we read that some who have been hospitable have unwittingly sheltered angels (13:2). Angels don't have wings. They can absolutely wear clothes.

What took place here was for Peter a miracle. He himself had done nothing to escape and there was nothing to be done. Here the Lord had intervened. For him walls, iron gates, and guard soldiers were no obstacles. Even when all is locked up, he cannot be locked out. The Lord can enter wherever he wishes. People and natural powers serve him when he wants to lead his own to freedom. In the prison at Philippi it was an earthquake that lifted the cell doors off their hinges and freed the two imprisoned messengers. It can be a political landslide or an amnesty or – as in the last war – an aerial bomb that ripped open a prison wall. I recall how Wolfgang Staemmler, the first supervisor of the electoral district, told with a grin how American soldiers freed him from prison and made him, as a Confessing Church pastor, the director of the prison in which his earlier guards now sat.

When God needs someone to spread the gospel, no wall is so thick, no castle so secure, no chain so strong, no guard so alert, no dictator so powerful – in a word, no obstacle so great that God cannot easily surmount it and set his messenger free.

The greatest hindrance to the expansion of the gospel are not autocrats like Herod or measures of intimidation against the church. The greatest hindrance is a church that avoids suffering, that gives away nothing and therefore must, regretfully, give in. Peter is not freed so that he could spend a few quiet years in some pleasant corner. To be sure, he disappears from the scene, he avoids the grasp of Herod, but he does not withdraw into private life. He does not say, "Just be careful now. Don't run any more risks!" He continues in the service of spreading the gospel until he also testifies to the truth of the gospel with his blood and glorifies God with his death.

III.

The Lord sees to it that the gospel spreads – through the suffering of his people, through the liberation of his people, and through the prayers of his people.

After James had been executed and Peter had been imprisoned, the church did not run around in panic. They had no other thought than going into hiding and, for heaven's sake, not to do anything to draw attention. Simply wait now until Herod settles down. No, they did not run around impetuously in a cold sweat, but rather they came together and prayed. "While Peter was kept in prison, the church prayed fervently to God for him," we read. When in the meantime Peter is freed and sets out for Mary's house, we are told that "many had gathered and were praying."

What were they praying for? For Peter's release from prison? "Lord, you know how very much we need him. You have ways and means to return him to us. How can we go on without him?" Such could have been their prayer. It would only be somewhat surprising if they did not believe the maid Rhoda when she reported, "Peter is standing outside." – "You are out of your mind!" they retorted. Should they really have expected so little from their prayer request? It could be. They would then be much like us when we pray so timidly and faint-heartedly, and rarely dare to hope that that for which we pray could actually happen. If that's the case, then from this story we should learn that God also does not spurn timid, needy, quiet prayers that are hardly audible, and that God always hears and understands them.

But perhaps they did not pray at all for Peter's release. Perhaps they prayed, "O Lord, you know what has happened to our brother Peter. If he should travel the same path as James, the path that leads to death, Lord, give him strength. Do not let him be confounded. Be near him. Take away all fear. May he remain steadfast and be your witness before the authorities. May he confess you who has taken away the power of death. May someone be moved to faith just as the centurion was who watched you die. And may we not be filled with fear and be silent, but instead give us courage and fearlessness. May we not hate those who persecute us so that the gospel may be proclaimed through us."

And maybe they added something like this: "If it is your will that our imprisoned brother continue once more on his journey with the gospel, then please find a way to free him from the hands of his captors. We do not know what your plan for him is. We only know that both possibilities – his witness by death or his release for a renewed witness – must be to serve the expansion of your glorious gospel that makes people happy and free."

Perhaps they concluded their prayer with something like this: And, Lord, if it is your will that we also should suffer for the sake of the gospel, may we not shirk from that suffering or bear it with heavy hearts. Guard us against bitterness toward those who do us harm, and also against self-pity. Instead, help us preserve the joy in our hearts that we have in you. That we are yours is enough for us. Amen.

# Romans 12:1-2
## May 23, 1984
### Bible study at the Gathering of the North German Church Assembly at the Hainstein Haus[55] in Eisenach

I appeal to you therefore, brothers and sisters, by the mercies of God, to present your bodies as a living sacrifice, holy and acceptable to God, which is your spiritual worship. Do not be conformed to this world, but be transformed by the renewing of your minds, so that you may discern what is the will of God – what is good and acceptable and perfect.

The worship service that the church celebrates is a continuation of the worship service that the church does in its life in the world. The liturgy after the liturgy, as the Orthodox say. Liturgy in the cultic space is absurd if it does not relate to this liturgy in the profane, everyday life. Celebratory worship in the church aims at worship in the quite uncelebratory world.

In the worship service in which we receive the gospel, we also receive strength, comfort, direction, and preparation for service in the world. The church is not a world unto itself. It is not some separate special world into which I may withdraw and leave behind the secular world in order to have at least an hour of rest. Rather, I take the world in which I live, which I embody, with me into worship, bringing its pain before God, seeking forgiveness for what I have done, solace for what I have suffered, strength and direction for what I need to be about in the world.

It is equally true that the secular world is not a world unto itself. It is not a world that is detached from God, a world in which the gospel has nothing to say. Instead, it is the world loved by God, the world in which the gospel will bring about changes that point in the

---

[55] Translator's note: Hainsain Haus is a hotel.

direction of God's kingdom and correspond to it. We are not citizens of two kingdoms, travelers between two worlds, nor are we like a pendulum swinging between church and world. The worship service in the church carries over into the service of God in the world.

It is an unfortunate narrow-mindedness that we Germans have become accustomed to using the phrase "worship service" exclusively for the gathering of the community in church. The community worships whenever it is assembled and hears God's word, prays, sings, whenever it celebrates the Lord's Supper.

What the community in all its members does elsewhere – vocationally, socially, at home – is clearly then not worship. Against this isolation this apostolic word speaks of that which we call worship, our life in the day-to-day world. Luther rightly understands the apostle when he says that the maid in the cow stall or the kitchen worships in the same sense as the pastor in the church. Luther was not at all wanting to diminish or exaggerate the gathering of the community to hear the gospel. Rather, he was returning dignity to the work of the church in the areas of secular life which it has, according to apostolic teaching: Because and insofar as it is done with loving devotion and in the hope for the new world, it is done in service to God to whom the world in all its areas of life belongs and who serves it in all places.

The apostle Paul and Martin Luther resist dividing the Christian life into two realms which have nothing or very little to do with each other – the sacred and the profane, the religious and the secular, the spiritual and the political realms.

No, the Christian life is a whole, and as a whole it is worship.

The apostle says to the church: the place of your worship is not the holy space, but rather the everyday reality of the world. The time of your worship is not the holy time on Sunday morning, but rather it is all time. The activities of your worship are not celebratory ceremonies, but rather your daily activities. The celebrants of your worship are not ordained clergy, but rather you, God's priestly people. Whenever we speak of the priesthood of all believers, that does not mean that all members of the church must be able to preach as needed, distribute the Lord's Supper, read the gospel, or engage in other churchly activities. What it means is that fundamentally all Christians carry out priestly functions as they make sacrifices, namely of themselves, as they offer their physical existence in the space of everyday reality, and so place themselves in the service of God to God's creation.

The priestly act of the believers does not consist of assuming the functions of the pastor when he or she is not there or assisting the pastor in celebrating the Lord's Supper, but rather of dedicating themselves as members of the new priestly people of God, giving themselves with all that they are to the events of the world, so that it does not destroy itself, so that the weak are not sacrificed to the strong, so that the world does not freeze in lovelessness, and so that they resist hopelessness. Right worship, the apostle says, takes place when we present our bodies as a living and holy sacrifice, our bodies – that's who we are, totally, with our gifts and our strengths, with what we have, and with what we can do, with our feelings and experiences – with everything God has given us, we, God's priestly people, are to give ourselves to God in grateful service to God's creation. God's gift makes possible and expects our devotion.[56] Because it is a matter of the devotion of those receiving the gift, there is not too much demanded of any of us. At stake is a living sacrifice which certainly is demanding but need not make us frantic.

A life lived with dedication, obedience, and responsibility is not a wasted life, but a victorious life. Jesus says, "For those who want to save their life will lose it, and those who lose their life for my sake, and for the sake of the gospel, will save it" (Mark 8:35).

The church's worship in the everyday world, therefore, is not simply engagement in world events, or random participation in political activities, or action for the sake of action. "Do not be conformed to this world" – that means, Do not accommodate yourselves to the fleeting world! Do not set your sights on what it declares to be reasonable, do not fall into line politically!

A politically aligned church that repeats blindly and uncritically public opinion or what the government says is letting the world enter its everyday life without worship. Also, a church that speaks

---

[56] Translator's note: Here Krusche plays on two words – Gabe (gift) and Hingabe (devotion or, literally, giving back).

protecting all sides so that everyone can appeal to her is guilty of worshiping the world. A church that wants to survive at any cost is already obsolete. A church that does not want to offend anyone is already completely tainted. "Do not be conformed to this world!"

In the Greek New Testament is the word "schema": Do not cooperate with the patterns (schema) of this world, do not adapt to this pattern (schema), to this system of behavior and norms. With that, there are certain ways of behavior that from the outset are excluded for the church.

The schema of this world is defined by two basic laws. The first is the law of reciprocity. With individuals it means, "Whatever you do to me, I'll do to you!" In politics it means, force will be met with force, threat with counter-threat. The other side must know that there will be a counter-blow. The more credible that the threat will be countered, all the more effective it is. One must therefore be prepared, as much as possible, to have a counter-threat ready. One would do well to see the other side as a potential criminal who is capable of anything and always ready to exploit one's own peaceful intentions. That is the logic of the world. The future that this opens is actually a continuation of the past, a story of blood, tears, and ruins. There's no creative impulse in it.

The second fundamental law of the world is the positive reversal of the first: the law of mutuality. I give to you, so that you will give to me. Thus, not blow and counter-blow, but gift and return gift, payment and equivalent return. Again, this has corollaries at both the individual and the governmental levels. I give something to someone with the expectation that that person will give me a corresponding gift. I help others with the hope that they will help me when I need it. More specifically, I will give to, and help, only those from whom I can with the greatest certainty expect the equivalent in return. Not their need, but their ability to help is what's decisive. The absurdity of this logic of the world consists in that it reduces all gifts and all assistance to refined forms of extortion, to a way of obligating me to others and making them dependent on me. All those who are poor who have nothing at all as equivalent gifts in this way remain either without assistance or their equivalent means giving up their freedom. They end up selling themselves. Aid for developing countries, then, is ascertained not on the basis of need, but on the adaptability of the recipient.

"Do not be conformed to this world!" Do not give in to this schema! Not adapt, but pay attention.[57] "Do not be conformed to this world, but be transformed by the renewing of your minds, so that you may discern what is the will of God – what is good and acceptable and perfect."

When we are "in Christ", our thinking is different. No longer do we accept uncritically the prevailing standards and values, but rather our thinking becomes markedly critical. "So that you may discern....." The church that engages in worship in the everyday world is by all means an unaccommodating, critical, and therefore disturbing force. It tests everything – arguments, assertions, stated goals, methods – that occurs in the everyday world. It does not reject everything and by no means does it consider everything that is thought, planned, and practiced in the world is bad. "Test everything; hold fast to what is good" (I Thess. 5:21). The standard is the will of God. It is not a matter of blanket judgments, but rather of a concrete distinction: What corresponds to the will of God, and what is contrary to it? What does God affirm, and what does God reject? What points in the direction of God's coming kingdom where justice and peace meet, and what is misguided? What serves the person who is loved by God and called to the freedom that God's children enjoy?

But now there is the unavoidable question: How does the church know what, in concrete terms, is the will of God, what conforms to God's will? The answer is this: The church has the gospel, the message, that in sending Jesus – his life, death, and resurrection – God has said the Yes of his love to this world that is estranged from God and fallen to death, and that God will free it from the powers of destruction and bring about the establishment of his kingdom of peace, in a life of full community with it. Clearly, the gospel is not a compendium of instructions for every conceivable situation in life in the everyday world. However, it is a call to responsibility and gives a clear basic orientation and criteria for decision-making for responsible living in the day-to-day world. And in the church of Jesus Christ there is the gift of prophecy which in critical situations makes so audible the voice of Christ that it is

---

[57] Translator's note: Here Krusche is employing a play on two German words: anpassen (to adapt) and aufpassen (to pay attention).

clear what it means, concretely, to do the will of God, what is acceptable to God, what is of service to people, and what the consequences are if God's will is ignored.

Today in our churches it has again become questionable the extent to which the gospel can lay claim beyond the realm of the personal to the realm of the social, political life. Not questionable is how the gospel influences the individual with its exhortation and encouragement calls him or her to repentance, to faith, and to discipleship. What is also not questionable is how the gospel works beyond the renewal of the person in the world of politics insofar as the conscience strengthens, the awareness of responsibility deepens, the sense of obligation is invigorated, the manner of interacting with each other is humanized.

This view is false the moment someone claims that the gospel is used only on a path of personal ambition in various life situations and the structures of the world, contributing nothing to the central issues themselves. The goal would be to change the persons in the institutions, not to change the institutions themselves.

Thus, the apostle Paul did not attack the system of slavery as such, but only admonished Christian slaves and slave owners, leaving their relationship and conduct toward each other to be defined by the gospel and thereby bringing about change in a more fundamental way. The realms of the economy and politics would have their own laws. The decisions as to the merits in these areas fall within the jurisdiction of the gospel.

But the gospel must take precautions against this displacement of the gospel from the arena of the political world into a private corner. Jesus Christ who is the head of every rule and authority (Col. 2:10), whom God has placed above all ruler and authority and power and dominion, and above every name and position (Eph. 1:20f.) cannot be reduced to Lord over hearts. The gospel cannot be reduced to the good news of salvation for the individual, but rather it is the good news of God's kingdom which has dawned in Jesus Christ and becomes fully real with his final coming. The church which is entrusted with the gospel of God's coming kingdom receives from it the chief criteria for its responsibility in the area of politics. In every decision it makes the church asks (and this helps individuals in carrying out their responsibilities): Does this resemble the kingdom of God? Does this point to God's coming kingdom of peace and justice and freedom? Does this reflect God's coming kingdom?

To be responsible for the gospel in the political world means asking these corresponding questions: Does this decision point in the direction of God's coming kingdom? As I make this decision, am I pointing to God's kingdom or am I disavowing it? As I make this decision, could someone believe that I am waiting for the coming of God's kingdom?

This morning we were asked to reflect on the question, "What can we do?" At the very least we can believe and hope that the kingdom of God is pulling history in its direction and to an open history, to a history with a future, to a history that is not simply an extension of the past. That is what we can do, namely, we can set up signals of this hope as we do not let our experiences of disappointment overwhelm us and therefore reject the statement: There is no point to it all. It is precisely this, that we do not utter this statement, that sets us apart from those who do not aspire to the kingdom of God. What we can do is ignite lights of hope in this often so dreary everyday world.

# II Corinthians 5:14-21
## March 28, 1986
### Good Friday at the Cathedral in Magdeburg

For the love of Christ urges us on, because we are convinced that one has died for all; therefore all have died. And he died for all, so that those who live might live no longer for themselves, but for him who died and was raised for them.

From now on, therefore, we regard no one from a human point of view; even though we once knew Christ from a human point of view, we know him no longer in that way. So if anyone is in Christ, there is a new creation; everything old has passed away; see, everything has become new! All this is from God, who reconciled us to himself through Christ, and has given us the ministry of reconciliation; that is, in Christ God was reconciling the world to himself, not counting their trespasses against them, and entrusting the message of reconciliation to us. So we are ambassadors for Christ, since God is making his appeal through us; we entreat you on behalf of Christ, be reconciled to God. For our sake he made him to be sin who knew no sin, so that in him we might become the righteousness of God.

Dear Friends! In our cathedral there's a cross on the altar. The cross stands on a sphere which is actually a globe of the world. In a tour of the cathedral by a class of students a young boy asked, "Why is there a plus sign above the globe?" Surely he was a young mathematician. He could not imagine the theological depth that lay behind his question: the cross, the plus sign above the world. The cross – a corresponding allusion to the notion that God sets the world not under a negative sign, but a positive one, that God does not say No, but Yes to the world. The world under the sign of the cross, the world reconciled by God with God. "In Christ God was reconciling the world to himself." Good Friday is World Reconciliation Day – an invitation to introduce us to the reconciliation that has already occurred, to the peace that has already been accomplished, to the magnificent new era. "Be reconciled to God!"

The first Good Friday did not take place in the church, but rather was brought about in the world. The cross on which Jesus hung stood not in the holy city, but outside the gate, in the filth of the earth. In the cross God reconciled the Christian to himself, so that the world does not succumb to its own filth. (We cannot close our eyes to the grim intransigence, the murderous enmity, the irreconcilable hostility that makes the image of our world into a dreadful grimace, disfigured by brutality and fear. And yet, we would look at the world with unbelief if we only saw it like that, if we were to see it without the raised cross in it, without the light of hope which falls from it on the world and on all of us. The world, as created by God – and as it therefore truly is –, is not the destructive world, but the world redeemed by God with God.) After Good Friday the world is not at all the same as it was before. In Christ it is reconciled with God, in it is planted "the word of reconciliation" which can no longer be silent and which today is proclaimed again.

**The cross of Good Friday – the event of world reconciliation.**

1. On the cross of Jesus Christ reconciliation is achieved.

2. From the cross of Jesus Christ the call goes out for reconciliation.

3. Beneath the cross of Jesus Christ reconciliation can be lived.

We could also talk in terms of ratified, proclaimed, and practiced reconciliation.

I.

On the cross of Jesus Christ reconciliation is achieved.

"In Christ God was reconciling the world to himself." The world of sinful people, of which we are all a part, therefore our world; the world of persons who would like to live without God and be their own lord, who are not able to understand why they should listen to God or thank God with their lives, who want to live from and for themselves, by their own strength and for their own purposes, and who thereby destroy their life and this world. Already in the opening pages the Bible shows us in an unvarnished way these persons who we are and whose image we do not enjoy looking at: the one who grasps at God's majesty and instead lays violent hands on his brother. The ungodly and thus brotherless person. So it is. The community gone kaputt among us is the inevitable consequence of our shattered relationship with God.

We and our world would be without hope if God simply left us alone, if God said, You want to live your life and have your world without me? Fine! If God were to say that, it would not be the reconciliation of the world, but its curse. The world abandoned by God would be the world given up to hopelessness.

But God did not abandon the world. "In Christ God was reconciling the world to himself." On the cross at Golgotha. On Good Friday we celebrate the fulfilled reconciliation of the world with God by God; the accomplished end of our enmity against God by God; the ratified peace treaty with us who rebelled against God's dominion – by God. "All this is from God," it says in our text. We have not contributed in the slightest to the act of reconciliation with God. If we had to expect something, it would be that God settle up with us. But the day of the great settlement of accounts became the day of the glorious reconciliation with us – by God.

God settled up, but in a most unusual way. All our transgressions and oversights, everything we did to God and to our neighbor or failed to do, all the harm we caused, whatever destructive forces we inflicted on the world and the lives of human beings, incessant and irreversible – all of that God has added up and taken into account. An enormous sum. But God did not assign all of that to our account; God did not burden us with it. "In Christ God was reconciling the world to himself, not counting their trespasses against them." God did not ascribe this overwhelming indictment to us, but rather to the one who was there entirely for God and entirely for humanity, and was wholly without sin.: "He made him to be sin who knew no sin." He did not settle accounts with us, but with himself. He did not let it cost us, but rather "he gave your dearest treasure."[58] On the cross of Christ all is settled with the world. Everything is put right. There is nothing more that stands between God and us. There is nothing left to do. God has made peace with us, with everyone of us. No one is left out. "God shows goodwill to one and all, and peace when troubled sinners all...."[59] Our sin hangs on the cross, there where Christ hangs. There is the end of what separated us, created by the world, there the world's claim on us and its power over us were lost.

The world after Good Friday: the world reconciled by God with God. It doesn't happen first by faith; it has happened before any faith.

But now the question can no longer be avoided as to whether this is not some pious theory, whether it is not some completely unrealistic claim. If the world is to be reconciled with God, how can there still be then so much rebellion against God, and how can there be murderous intransigence, hatred and enmity in the world that confront us daily and against which we feel so powerless?

In the November 23, 1953 issue of the Frankfurter Allgemeine Zeitung[60] there appeared the following: "On the small Pacific island of Guam ten Japanese soldiers were still fighting the war. At the request of the Japanese government American sea and air forces are now trying to convince them that an armistice had been concluded more than eight years earlier."

The same is true with the great day of reconciliation. Reconciliation has been ratified. The conclusion of peace is in effect. But there are those who haven't heard anything about the fact that God has made peace with the world and has extended his hand. And there are others who have indeed heard this, but who do not believe this news and therefore continue to struggle against God and with each other and take shelter before God. Although the following is true,

---

[58] Translator's note: Line from Martin Luther's hymn "Nun freut euch, lieben Christen g'mein" ("Dear Christians, One and All Rejoice" in the Evangelical Lutheran hymnal Worship, #594).
[59] Translator's note: Line from Nikolaus Decius' hymn "Allein Gott in der Höhe sei" ("All Glory Be to God on High" in the Evangelical Lutheran hymnal Worship, #410).
[60] Translator's note: Major newspaper out of Frankfurt, Germany. The translation is mine.

On the cross of Jesus Christ reconciliation is achieved, the second point is necessary:

## II.

From the cross of Jesus Christ the call goes out for reconciliation.

The world is reconciled with God, whether it believes it or not. That can no longer be undone. From God's side everything that stood in the way of peace with God has been swept clean. In the crucified Christ God's hand is extended to us and has gripped us. And there are enough people whose entire happiness consists in being grasped by this hand, from which they had for so long withdrawn, grasped by the "hand that does not let go." I believe we belong to them, to the church of those who are reconciled with God. But because we believe – for ourselves and others: We are reconciled with God, we have peace with God – we are at the same time made ambassadors to those who have either not yet heard this message or who do not yet believe that it is really true.

"So we are ambassadors for Christ, since God is making his appeal through us; we entreat you on behalf of Christ, be reconciled to God." Naturally, it is easy to say from the pulpit, but how do we say that to an individual? The simplest is an encounter with someone who has been consumed with what he or she has caused in the life of another – through ambition or carelessness or meanness – and has caused pain. Or an encounter with someone who has become alarmingly aware that his or her life up to now has always revolved around self so that success was all that mattered, and now no longer wished to live. To such persons we are able to say, It's true. What you have done with your life or have caused in the life of another is bad. Be happy that you recognize that and do not want to excuse it. But God does not want things to stay as they are and for you to be burdened with forever. That is why God has taken it away from you and removed it altogether. No longer must it hang around your neck; now it hangs where Christ hangs. Now let it stay there.

"In Christ God was reconciling the world to himself, not counting their trespasses against them." – "Not counting their trespasses against them." Here all persons may leave their burdens. "I have played with a human life – played irresponsibly" – and not counting their trespasses against them. "I have been blind to the pain of someone very close to me; I did not realize how difficult life was for him. I feel guilty that he was no longer able to bear it alone." – and he did not count their trespasses against them."I was silent when they attacked and killed him. I am to blame for his bitterness" – not counting their trespasses against them. "I broke up another marriage"; "In anger I lost myself and struck my son"; "I stole another's property"; "I passed on nasty gossip about someone"; not counting their trespasses against them. He takes them from us and takes them on himself. And therefore, "Be reconciled to God." As I said earlier, it is relatively easy to tell others that their guilt is taken away.

It is much more difficult to share the words, "Be reconciled with God" to someone who continues to feel guilty toward another. Perhaps the invitation to accept God's forgiveness might sound something like this: For goodness sake, stop feeling so guilty toward others! You are only cultivating a hard heart, and your outlook does get any more attractive. Surely others also have their own guilt. But God has already cared for them, having forgiven them. Yours too, by the way. And now you need not waste your time worrying – about your own shortcomings or those of others. Leave it up to God. God has made peace with you and with others. Now stop the war. You will notice that life is much better that way.

It is also very difficult to issue the invitation "Be reconciled to God" to those who always talk about how much good they do. Oh, they have a few flaws, but they are of the opinion that, if everyone were more like them, the world would look a bit different. Why is it then necessary for him to be reconciled to God?

Perhaps we would have to say to them that by looking at ourselves we are not quite so sure. If we were to look at our lives, this is clear: we cannot escape God. Even on our good days God sees how much vanity and how much calculation is at play. Above all, God sees how much good we have neglected to do. The guilt of love that remains guilty weighs so heavily on one of us – certainly on me – that only God was able to bear it and remove it from the world.

We will say that to others with love, not insultingly, not condescendingly, not with pressure, not priest-like, certainly not threateningly, and not at all in terms of the Last Judgment. "We entreat you on behalf of Christ, be reconciled to God." We should ask them not on our knees or in a manipulative way or by forcing the issue.

We cannot do this as if we hear the words "Be reconciled to God" only for others and as if we ourselves do not need to hear them. In view of the intransigence of the world we cannot, unfortunately, point to ourselves and say, Look at us – that's how the reconciled live! Our stubbornness opposite those who are not like us – and among the pious of varying character there is an irreconcilability that is no less comparable to that that governs the world –, our own stubbornness towards our invitation, unfortunately, is influenced by the world's overwhelming strength. This should not deject us, but should make us humble and modest.

**From the cross of Jesus Christ the call goes out for reconciliation** – and this call is aimed at us also –, and so we come to the third point in this text:

III.

**Beneath the cross of Jesus Christ reconciliation can be lived.**

On the cross of Christ our sinful, old self also died. It no longer has any claim on us. Christ, the new person, has full claim on us. "If one has died for all," writes the apostle, "therefore all have died. And he died for all, so that those who live might live no longer for themselves, but for him who died and was raised for them."

Brothers and sisters, through the death of Christ our life has a new beginning. We are dead to the life that revolves around us; now we want to live for him who died and rose for us. We are no longer in the center of our life; he is the new center. To live for him, to let our life be defined by him means being there for those whom he loves, for his poor brothers and sisters. Whoever no longer exists for themselves but exists in Christ, whoever therefore is reconciled with God and has become a new creation, that person has a new relationship with others. "From now on, therefore, we regard no one from a human point of view," we read here. That means that from now on we judge no one according to the old standards – that is, no longer according to whether or not he or she harms us or uses us, whether or not he or she restricts us or enriches us, whether or not he or she stands in our way, or whether or not we move on in spite of him or her (move on spiritually is understood). If we are reconciled with God in Christ, then such standards and their corresponding behavior toward others have become obsolete, feeble, and unacceptable. We then see others in the light of Christ: equally lost, equally loved, equally reconciled, called to the same life of excellence. With Christ we no longer let anything tarnish this crucial outlook.

To live out of this reconciliation with God, to live lives of reconciliation in a world of intransigence does not at all mean being timid or going along with injustice, oppression, exploitation, or not opposing anything, supposing oneself in opposition and fleeing to some kind of neutrality. But to practice reconciliation well means opposition not becoming enmity, not returning hate with hate, and then when there is discussion to stand up for justice for the weaker ones and unflinchingly keep the goal in mind that a common life is again possible. Practicing reconciliation is for relationships in larger contexts as well as for those in individual relationships: taking the first step just as Jesus took the first step when we were still enemies. The first step is always a risky one, but with each such step we conform to the reconciliation fulfilled on Good Friday.

In a moment we will celebrate Holy Communion, the meal of reconciliation with God and with each other and with great hope for all who are invited: "Be reconciled with God!" Amen.

# Galatians 5:1-6
## October 31, 1988
### Reformation Day Celebration in Würzburg[61]

For freedom Christ has set us free. Stand firm, therefore, and do not submit again to a yoke of slavery. Listen! I, Paul, am telling you that if you let yourselves be circumcised, Christ will be of no benefit to you. Once again I testify to every man who lets himself be circumcised that he is obliged to obey the entire law. You who want to be justified by the law have cut yourselves off from Christ; you have fallen away from grace. For through the Spirit, by faith, we eagerly wait for the hope of righteousness. For in Christ Jesus neither circumcision nor uncircumcision counts for anything; the only thing that counts is faith working through love.

Dear Friends, "For freedom Christ has set us free!" That sounds like a fanfare flourish. And there have been times in our church, particularly in celebrating the Reformation, when such a fanfare flourish was especially powerful. At such times Luther was praised as the man who boldly and without fear confronted the emperor and pope in "The Freedom of a Christian"[62]. The Reformation as the great freedom movement which frees us from the yoke of clerical control, dogma pressure, and ecclesiastical tutelage, brought us spiritual freedom and freedom of conscience, and introduced the emancipation of people from ignorance and being treated like children. Such an arrogant voice is long since past. We have too painfully seen how distant we are from the freedom of which one could sing: "Let goods and kindred go, This mortal life also; the body they may kill...."[63]

---

[61] Translator's note: Würzburg is a city in the former West Germany.
[62] Translator's note: This is a treatise Luther wrote in 1520 to Pope Leo X.
[63] Translator's note: From Luther's hymn "A Mighty Fortress Is Our God".

Today, however, discussions of freedom are quite different, though with no less self-assurance, namely, in the arena of politics. The western world lays claim to this word almost exclusively for itself. With clear pathos she calls herself the free world in contrast to that from which I come, in which I live, and over against which it wants to defend its freedom – if necessary, with atomic weapons. (Freedom takes absolute priority over peace.)

Now it happens that I, from the un-free world, am supposed to speak to you (publicly, free people) precisely about freedom (I didn't choose the sermon text for today!). But as a preacher of the gospel I will not speak about freedom in general, but about the freedom we are invited to consider that Christ gave us and revealed as a new possibility for living.

"For freedom Christ has set us free" – the apostle reminds the church of that. It is the freedom that Christ reveals to her as the common freedom of all who cannot live for themselves alone, but which they can always have together with others, never without it, never against it.

**We are the church of people freed by Christ:**

1. freed to a life that comes from God,

2. freed to live a life for others.

I.

**Freed to live a life that comes from God**

If it is Jesus that frees us, then that means that without him none of us is free, prisoners controlled by someone else – whether we live in the so-called free world or somewhere else. Furthermore, that means that we ourselves are not in a position to escape this captivity. Indeed, without him we don't even notice it. "So if the Son makes you free, you will be free indeed" (John 8:36), Jesus said to people who were particularly proud of their freedom and reacted indignantly to the idea that they needed to be freed.

Only when Jesus comes into our life with his liberating power do we begin to see that and in what kind of captivity we had been living. The Bible calls it a life dominated by sin, a life that shut itself off from God, that left God outside. It is the life of the homo **incurvatus in se ipsum**, as Luther formulated it: the life that turns inward on itself, that is entangled with itself, the person that, in spite of all booms and busts, always returns to self; the person who, without God, wants to live on one's own – from oneself and for oneself – and who lives either by the dictum, You should enjoy your life! or by the imperative, You must make something of your life! In either case such persons fall under an unyielding law which will dominate them, namely, the law of greed that drives them: take what you can get, don't let go of anything, enjoy everything to the fullest, don't renounce anything. Or they succumb to the law of achievement which means merciless pressure: be successful, follow through, climb the ladder, justify your life, be seen as legitimate by what you accomplish.

How un-free such a life is can be seen in how it is characterized by constant worry, worry about danger, worry about possible loss of standard of living and accumulated wealth, worry about one's reputation and one's outer appearance, worry about loss of influence and loss of power. Such a life of complete captivity is especially seen in a constant fear of death which either intensifies selfishness – "Let us eat and drink, for tomorrow we die" (Isaiah 22:13) (the slogan of those who fear death) – or it leads to a flight from the hard reality of our mortality into senseless work or into the nebulousness of Far Eastern religiosity.

Jesus Christ has freed us from this self-entangled, self-absorbed, self-created life that is filled with dependency and fear. To those who live under the law of greed, he says, You cannot constantly hide behind your life, you need not be afraid, you could come up short, cheating life if you don't have everything others have. You cannot always long for life and selfishly seize everything that the world so tantalizingly offers, and yet you still come up empty. "I am the bread of life" (John 6:35), Jesus says. If you let me into your life and let me dwell there, you will experience me in your whole being so that you will live, lacking nothing, even if you don't have much. "I came that they may have life, and have it abundantly" (John 10:10b), life in its fullness, life that lacks nothing, life that keeps us and which no one can take from us, not even death. The loveliest part always lies before us: eternal communion with God with unimaginable joy. "For freedom Christ has set us free," free from the pressure of needing to manage our own lives, free to see life as a gift from God, to live life in him.

To the others whose lives are governed by the law of achievement, Jesus says, You don't have to make something of yourselves. A long time ago God made something of you, namely, the most splendid thing possible: God's children – God's sons and daughters. With God you are at home. Everything that belongs to God is yours as well. Your life is free from having to legitimize yourself by anything you may achieve. You don't have to train your children mercilessly to perform. Your life is not worthless if you cannot achieve anything more. You don't have to create who you are; you only need to live who, in reality, you already are: God's sons and daughters in the free air of your Father's house. Self-realization, therefore, becomes a senseless word. God does not love you because of what you can do; God created you out of boundless love. Those who cannot achieve are also loved. You live out of a love that cost everything for you: God's son gave his own life. So, to be loved by him – that is our freedom.

If I am loved by him, I also know that there is nothing I have done to earn this love, that it is not motivated by anything in me. There is a sentence from Martin Luther in the Heidelberg Disputation which I especially like. He says there: "Sinners are good because they are loved; they are not loved because they are good."[64] If we are indebted to God because of God's unearned love, we no longer have to make ourselves good, but rather we are free to confess honestly our guilt – the guilt of failing to love, the unspoken word, broken faith, refusal to help, the angry gossip – free to renounce and confess all attempts to excuse ourselves: I am guilty. I alone, and no other. I can confess that because I belong to the one who has taken away the burden of my guilt and has taken it to the cross. He has freed me from this oppressive burden. I am in debt to him

---

[64] Translator's note: In The Essential Luther Tryntje Helfferich translates this passage: "Therefore sinners are beautiful because they are esteemed; they are not esteemed because they are beautiful" (p. 46 under paragraph 28).

who loves me with an unbounded love and an undeserved love. I am totally in debt to his grace. Whoever is absolutely indebted to his grace is a free person – in the church of persons freed by Christ. **Freed to live a life that comes from God**. And:

II.

**Freed to live a life for others**

The freedom to live absolutely and only by grace is not at all easily lived out. It appears to be so simple. The apostle struggles against the danger of freedom and the preservation of freedom: "For freedom Christ has set us free. Stand firm, therefore, and do not submit again to a yoke of slavery." At the time Paul was dealing with people who were saying to the church: Of course the grace of Jesus Christ is crucial. But a heathen (a non-Jew) cannot simply receive, merely by baptism, the grace of Jesus Christ. That person must still first meet one condition, namely, he must be circumcised. Grace, yes, but not without something more, not for me and not for you. The person must do something more.

Here everything is at stake for Paul: grace in its freedom. Grace is either free and unconditional, or it is not grace. Whoever talks of "worthiness of grace" has nothing and has not understood anything. None of us is worthy of grace, and yet all of us are in need of it. Whoever makes grace dependent on assumptions or conditions, on any kind of worthiness, to them the apostle says, "You have cut yourselves off from Christ; you have fallen away from grace." You have returned to the prison of your graceless mentality of works. Either Christ alone, grace alone – or you are alone with yourself.

"For in Christ Jesus neither circumcision nor uncircumcision counts for anything; the only thing that counts is faith working through love." Whatever advantage one may have over another, what gifts one has or doesn't have, whether one has a religious upbringing or an atheistic one, whether one is baptized Protestant or Catholic, whether one lives in the west or in the east – in God's eyes that is irrelevant. The only thing that matters is faith in God's boundless love, or, which is the same, it only matters if I welcome into my life Jesus in whom one finds God's unencumbered love, God's free grace, that is, if I believe. The decisive difference between human beings is not what they do, but whether they believe, whether it is enough for their lives: we are loved, boundlessly loved – by grace. We owe all that we are to this love.

This faith is not our action, but it makes us active. It rests on the activity of the love of God in Jesus Christ, and it is prompted to be shared by the love it received. It is "faith working through love," as stated here. This love does not come in addition to faith, but rather is part of it. Faith is bound up with love, and they interact with each other.

A life lived in love is a life lived for others. We don't simply have this freedom to live for others if it is seen as only when we want to; rather, we have this freedom to live for others when our life stands at Christ's disposal. At the outset this freedom is at its root distinguished from the freedom a normal citizen understands and from that which is found in the Universal Declaration of Human Rights: "Freedom which I mean" – the freedom of the individual. One should shape one's life according to one's needs, talents, and interests, and be able to expand freely in every direction – intellectually, morally, and, above all, economically –, so that one is true to oneself. (In addition, belonging to this freedom is the right given to everyone to keep in mind what is to one's own benefit.)

Because freedom is understood in this way – as my individual freedom – others only come secondarily, as an afterthought, as those with the same claim to freedom to limit my freedom, standing in my way, keeping me from fully exercising my freedom, and against whom I must assert and guard myself. Others are rivals to my freedom. This kind of freedom mobilizes my need to achieve, but at the same time it drives me to be successful against others, to outdo them. Understood this way, the freedom of the individual becomes the freedom of the strong to swing elbows, the freedom to strive for success and power. Those with a weaker constitution, with worse social connections, with thinner skin and not so well-developed elbows end up on the edges of liberal society. (If I were preaching today in the German Democratic Republic, I would have to point out how there the collectivism undervalues the freedom of the individual, the freedom to think independently and share responsibility maturely. But I am here preaching on this text.)

"For freedom Christ has set us free" – to live for others. Christ gives me the openness to see others. He does not come into my vision as an afterthought, but as soon as I open my eyes – and not at all as one who curtails my freedom, but as one who makes my freedom real. The other is not a border fence, but is a field where my freedom is exercised and tested. The faith that is working through love lets me see others in a completely new way: they are not ones against whom I must contend, against whom I must prove myself right, but rather they are the ones who need people and who accept them. I can see them as those against whom I do not need to flex my muscles or raise my fist, but ones who need an outstretched hand. To be free to see others with eyes of love means to see them as persons for whom Christ died. It means asking, What are they going through? How should I approach them? How might I be seen by them? How might I be changed by this encounter? Living for others, living by faith working through love leaves no one the same. They are moved by the question, What do others need from me?

If Jesus Christ has freed me for freedom, to live a life of love, then I do well to orient myself to him. What kind of freedom to love makes him visible! He sits at the table with those who truly do not have the finest manners, with those for whom the self-righteous have only disparaging remarks, and they insult him, calling him a glutton and a boozer, associating with the most annoying people because he knew that he could only help them not by turning up his nose at them, but by opening up his heart to them – just as he behaved toward lepers, to those who have been ostracized by society as dangerous carriers of infections. As he lifted the barriers to contact and met with them without any fear of touching them, healed them, he enabled them to re-enter society, and thereby helped them become integral members of society.

He was free to become part of the civil and ecclesiastical structures out of love, but he was just as free, also out of love, to break through them if it meant helping those who were suffering. A royal freedom! Freedom for the weak, the neglected, the passed over, those shoved to the margins. The freedom no longer to have to ask, What will become of me if I help this person? but rather, What will happen to this person if I do nothing? No longer, Why me? but, If not me, then who?

Dear brothers and sisters, here in the west you have many enviable freedoms. But having these freedoms does not make free people or a free society. Freedom is no more the sum of all freedoms than God is the collective sum of all gods. These freedoms are only enjoyed humanly by those who are already free, freed by Christ from the pressure of having to live a life to the fullest at the expense of others, and freed from the pressure of having to live a life of achievement without regard for others; free to use one's own freedom to enhance the freedom of others, out of freedom free to waive freedoms.

The church of persons freed by Christ is God's counter-movement against the perversions of freedom, against its ruin by libertinism or its degeneracy by power plays, and it is also God's counter-movement against the rejection of freedom. God desires that we, whom God has freed from ourselves for a life of love, react with great sensitivity, attentively, and crying out wherever someone loved by God is held captive, degraded as an object of greed or interests, stepped on, pressed against the wall, mistreated, or exploited.

"For freedom Christ has set you free." Not only does that sound like a fanfare flourish, but it is also arouses us anew to the splendid freedom of the children of God that is given to us through Jesus Christ, a freedom that radiates through us to be effective in a world of misused and rejected freedom, a world whose only hope is the kingdom of eternal freedom that Christ brings, and in which we may be like him, and thus be unhindered and undiminished – God's free children as those in this worship service he now invites to his table for renewal and strengthening of community with him. Amen.

# I Thessalonians 4:1-8
## October 19, 1980
### 20th Sunday after Trinity Sunday in the Cathedral in Magdeburg

Finally, brothers and sisters, we ask and urge you in the Lord Jesus that, as you learned from us how you ought to live and to please God (as, in fact, you are doing), you should do so more and more. For you know what instructions we gave you through the Lord Jesus. For this is the will of God, your sanctification: that you abstain from fornication; that each one of you know how to control your own body in holiness and honor, not with lustful passion, like the Gentiles who do not know God; that no one wrong or exploit a brother or sister in this matter, because the Lord is an avenger in all these things, just as we have already told you beforehand and solemnly warned you. For God did not call us to impurity but in holiness. Therefore whoever rejects this rejects not human authority but God, who also gives his Holy Spirit to you.

Dear Friends! Some time ago I wrote a letter to a colleague because I had become aware that his marriage was in jeopardy as he had become involved with another woman. I wrote him saying that I thought it necessary for us to discuss this. He wrote back, very politely, that this was a private matter and that he did not want to discuss it with me; he did not want to let anyone into his intimate world.

Of course! Quite honestly, I would not want to share with everyone my personal issues. There are those obtrusive persons who think they always have to meddle. But for one whom I know belongs to Jesus Christ and takes that seriously and have his life defined by him, for such a person I would allow certain things in my life to be addressed. I know that I need and would like for God to have a bit of joy in my life, and a bit more.

The people who belonged to the church in Thessalonica obviously did not regard as unwanted meddling in their privacy the apostle Paul's very direct response to some definite questions regarding their personal conduct. It is quite apparent that they noticed that here no moral preacher or school master was speaking to them, pointing a pedagogical finger at them, speaking from a raised platform, but rather a brother who, as they did, wanted to lead his life before God, under God's eyes, and in obedience to God's commandment. He does not rebuke them, but rather tells them directly that they are on the right path and therefore asks and exhorts them to stay on this path and continue to progress on it.

"You learned from us how you should live to please God; and you are living so. Now we ask and urge you in the name of Jesus to make further progress," it says in the "Good News" translation.[65] "For that is the will of God, that you live holy lives." God would like for our whole life to belong to him, conform to him, bearing ourselves in like manner, and reflecting something of that in our everyday relationships.

God's way became clear in Jesus Christ as the way that does not seek for self but for others; that seeks not one's own happiness but the happiness of others; that does not come thinking of self, but gives everything for the sake of others. This way should be the way for us and for the church more and more as opposed to our natural and selfish ways which are repugnant to God. It doesn't happen all at once – that's why we talk of having to make progress. And it doesn't happen from within. There always needs to be in the church those who admonish and encourage others, and can discredit any who tend to browbeat, morally, or who pretentiously oversee others, or who are not willing to stand with the admonished in the community of the Lord Jesus and under his sovereign authority; in short, those who want to be their own master. Whoever wants to be their own master must naturally not put up with any admonitions.

This way of Jesus will take shape in every aspect of our life, even in our most intimate life. One need not be a Freudian to acknowledge that our gender, our sexuality indisputably determines and shapes our life to a considerable degree. That is why this important life

---

[65] Translator's note: Translated from the German Die Gute Nachricht.

complex may not remain outside if we want to subordinate our life to God and have it defined by God.

I.

So, what does it mean to live a holy life, to live in such a way that it corresponds to God's way when it comes to the relationship between husband and wife?

First answer: **To want completely and forever to be for each other**. I could also put it this way: **To meet the other as friend**.[66]

"For this is the will of God, your sanctification: that you abstain from fornication." We recognize the Greek word that is used here – porneia – in a somewhat modified form, we speak of pornography. That does not simply have to do with sexuality. Some people cannot imagine the church doing anything other than setting up large "Forbidden" signs when it comes to the entire subject of sexuality and love relationships between husband and wife. Clearly, they are under the impression that God is an old grump who would not want them to talk about love or share images of the body with others: like a raging sea or a calming wind. Quite unjustified is the suspicion that the church has a broken relationship with sexuality. Christian upbringing and piety have, in fact, often instilled more fears about human sexuality than joy and affirmation. "Everything with as little pleasure as possible" seems to be the maxim of Christian sexual morality.

I ask myself how we could have come to this point. Did the Creator who formed humanity as husband and wife, and who desires that they blend with each other as "one flesh", a most intimate unity – did the Creator count on them ruining their sexual relationship, bringing it into discredit, distrusting it as a sin, wanting to make it as unimportant as possible?

In the verbatim of a conversation which the writer Maxi Wander developed literarily, various vocations and interests of women are reported, sharing information about their life as a spouse. There

---

[66] Translator's note: In German, literally, it addresses the other as Du (the informal, familiar of "you") as opposed to the more formal Sie.

Rosi, 32 years old, a secretary and married with one child, says, "I believe I have my husband in my blood. I cannot imagine being with another man." A bit later in this record we read, "I do not belong with those women who think they can be happy with only one man. I constantly meet men who please me.... One must simply make a choice. And then he will be the only one that makes one happy. I do not tend toward passionate outbursts. I am curious, I am restless, I am like a child, my husband says. And I say that I have few inhibitions. I will not live with any other man or confide my innermost thoughts with another man.... Something occurs to me that you may find odd. We all gulp this green pill at breakfast which has made us free. I know for sure that I am not running any risks. But do you know what? If I love my husband, I want to run this risk. Something important is left out, a great shock. Without this risk one feels flat. For me sex is not only fun, but it is something total. In sex I express my whole personality, much more directly than anywhere else." That is clearly not a Christian who says that, but it is so honest, so open, so uninhibited, and yet it is also said without the slightest trace of shamelessness and is delivered with such a sense of wholeness that a Christian could well have said it.

"For this is the will of God, your sanctification; that you abstain from fornication." To live a holy life in the relationship of husband and wife means to live in such a way that something of God's way is reflected. God's way is that God sets up an I-You relationship between God and us, a communion of love in which God devotes God's self wholly to us, giving God's self completely to us. The communion of love in which husband and wife encounter each other and give self to the other, is not based on sexuality; it is much richer than that. Sexuality in included in the wholeness of the relationship.

"Fornication" – porno – is the monster of sexuality which has been taken out of the totality of the meaning of love and has established its own independence. Fornication – porno – is a sexual relationship that involves no commitment to the other person, that wants to assume no residual responsibility for the other, that is satisfied with one night, that wants to keep open all options. For her, the other is no longer interesting as a committed partner in his physical-spiritual wholeness, no longer the heart, but only what is between his legs, a sexual relationship in which the other is replaceable, as uninteresting after pleasure as an empty box of candy. A sexual relationship that takes place outside the bond of marriage or at least does not aim at this bond, on the contrary, does not consciously accept responsibility for the other for the rest of one's life, is a porno relationship. Not because sexual pleasure is bad, but because selfishness is bad when it makes the other a consumer product.

"Without responsibility it doesn't work," Rosi the secretary mentioned. That is a key word. If someone says, "I would like to sleep with you," and then to the question, "Would you also like to grow old with me?" answers with a foolish expression, it's clear what he wants, namely, the other not as a loved person, but as a desirable sexual object. In any case, one should not call that love.

The porno relationship, the sex-trafficking (this hideous phrase today), which removes the commitment from I-You, is already common among sixteen-year-olds. I do not say that judgmentally or as someone who is omniscient or who is angry. The sixteen-year-olds today are not worse than we were at that age. It simply hurts me to see them waste this gift and their spirit and no longer be capable of a greater love. Precisely because God gives us the gift of sexuality, God intends it to be wrapped in a relationship of love in which each wants to belong to the other completely, exclusively, and forever. Only in that way can the gift of sexuality be experienced in a happy and enriched way because they now form a wonderful wholeness that includes the many other gifts God has given us.

"For this is the will of God, your sanctification: that you abstain from fornication." Do not let your sexuality wander around loosely and irresponsibly. Instead, give it its place in a life-time relationship in which you want to be there for each other, body and soul.

## II.

The second answer to the question, "What does it mean to live a holy life in view of the loving relationship between husband and wife?" is, **To honor the dignity of the other.**

"Each one of you should know how to control your own body in holiness and honor[67], not with lustful passion, like the Gentiles who do not know God." The selfishness that is only interested in its own gratification is expressed not only in unconditional sleeping around, but it also threatens the life of the marriage. I would like to mention my own experience, even at the expense of another's spiritual and physical health. There are a man's claims that take the honor of the wife, harming and humiliating her in a most profound way.

I have heard from an experienced divorce judge that a very common reason given for the motion for divorce are a husband's demands which are considered by the wife as shameless, harmful to her inner dignity, and rape. Respect in a marriage means having regard for the other's feelings, the other's frame of mind – and this consideration is especially for the wife – discretion, tenderness, and tact. One cannot simply know this; it must be learned. "Each one must live with his own wife in holiness and honor." Here there is much to learn, always discovering something new that pleases her, helps her flourish, contributes to her beauty. What's to be learned here is, above all, what's to let go of. A husband must not force himself on his wife. I have no claims or rights to assert. Whoever does not want to learn to respect, to practice restraint and self-control, to subdue his sexuality will experience a shipwreck whenever his wife becomes ill and simply cannot fulfill his desires.

As old-fashioned as it may sound, "Each of you must learn to live with his own wife in holiness and honor, not with lustful passion, like the Gentiles" – it is not at all antiquated. The former president of our Synod, Lother Kreyssig, once wrote us in a letter how his wife had suffered from dementia, such that for a long period of time she had not recognized him. However, he spoke of his wife with such love, esteem, and kindness that something of her earlier beauty and inner richness radiated again and again. That could not have happened if he had not learned early on to live with his wife with kindness and honor – learned from his relationship with Jesus who always honored the weak and treated such persons with dignity in their weakness.

---

[67] Translator's note: The German of this phrase is "live with his own wife in holiness and honor" which is a variant that is mentioned in the NRSV.

## III.

The **third answer** in the text to the question, "What does it mean to live a holy life in view of the loving relationship between husband and wife?" is, **To have regard for the marriage of a weaker person or for the weaker person in a marriage.**

"No one wrong or exploit a brother or sister in this matter." Here it seems that a whole new theme is raised. The business of sexuality[68]. The Greek word here can, in fact, mean "business." But it can also simply mean "concern, matter." Then the apostle says, "No one wrong or exploit a brother or sister in this matter, namely, one's love life." To live a holy life in view of the loving relationship between husband and wife means, I respect the marriage of the other. For me, this is an indisputable boundary.

For someone who is either in an unhappy marriage or who is unhappy being alone, there is always the great temptation to find the weakness in another marriage, exploit it, and take advantage of it, as it says here: supplant or disparage one of the marriage partners. Perhaps it happens that one demonstrates his vitality over against the sick person or displays his sparkling personality over against the disadvantaged brother and thereby collects points with the wife whose unhappiness he has clearly noticed. But the same could actually be said of the wife, namely, that she shows off her beauty against the less attractive sister, her cleverness against the somewhat helpless sister, so that she will gain the admiration of the husband whose signals of sympathy she picked up on a long time ago. Also, whoever persuades themselves that they only want to take care of a misunderstood, unhappy spouse who comes off badly in a marriage, is taking advantage of the weak spouse whose marriage is falling apart. The help of the one who lives an upright life, who wants to live in the way of Jesus Christ, would have to look very different here. That person would have to try to point out the strengths of the other.

"For God did not call us to impurity but in holiness." To that end we are to reflect something of God's way, God's loving gift of

---

[68] Translator's note: Krusche's phrase is "nach der Geschlechtlichkeit die Geschäftlichkeit".

wholeness to humanity in all parts of our life, even in the area of loving relationships of husband and wife.

Perhaps we have noticed that God does not condemn our inadequacy here, but instead brings us full happiness, not hemming us in, but leading us into freedom – into the freedom of being ourselves and thus into the freedom for the beloved other person. Amen.

# Hebrews 4:14-16
## February 16, 1986
### 1st Sunday in Lent in the Cathedral at Magdeburg

Since, then, we have a great high priest who has passed through the heavens, Jesus, the Son of God, let us hold fast to our confession. For we do not have a high priest who is unable to sympathize with our weaknesses, but we have one who in every respect has been tested as we are, yet without sin. Let us therefore approach the throne of grace with boldness, so that we may receive mercy and find grace to help in time of need.

Dear Friends! The Heidelberg Catechism opens with the question, "What is your only comfort in life and in death?" The answer is, "That I am not my own, but belong – body and soul, in life and in death – to my faithful Savior, Jesus Christ." Brothers and sisters, who can say that! My whole comfort and my entire happiness are found in the fact that I belong to him, that I belong to Jesus Christ. I am his – that says everything that is important about me. I am to be considered only together with him. There are quite surely some among us who could say that of themselves. Good for them! They would gladly concede that this certainty was not always in their life and is not always there now.

Some among us who have a relationship with Jesus Christ would perhaps speak a bit more cautiously about it. They still have painful memories, as weak as their faith was, when it came to depending completely on him – Jesus Christ – and surrendering everything to him. They are also not sure that they would acknowledge confessing Jesus Christ and join his church, if push came to shove. Sometimes they pose the question whether it can be true that all power in heaven and on earth is given to him. And yet, they think that they are no longer separated from him. Something was triggered in them. Somehow they will need him again and again.

On this first Sunday in Lent it is impressed on us what our relationship with Jesus Christ may look like in particular:

**In Jesus Christ we have the one we need.**

1. He is tempted as we are.

2. He knows our weaknesses.

3. We can come to him any time.

I.

**In Jesus Christ we have the one we need. He is tempted as we are.**

We need someone who understands us, who knows what it means to be human. A Son of God who only appears to be human, who would not have been human with all the consequences of that, who would not really only appear to have been tempted, would be of no help to us at all. But Jesus Christ was not such a one. "He had to become like his brothers and sisters in every respect" (Heb. 2:17), as he is described. Then in our passage, "in every respect tested as we are." For me, that is the most important thing that is said about Jesus. That makes him close to me: in everything like us. In every respect tempted as we are.

His temptations were no pretense. From the outset it was not certain that he would resist them. In the Gospel reading for this Sunday we heard of the temptations to which Jesus was subjected at the beginning of his ministry. By no means were these the only ones. As in these, it was always a matter of diverting Jesus from a path that would end at the cross, of taking him in a direction that would avoid the cross. The voice of temptation was always there: you don't have to take this path. All temptations tried to move Jesus to preserve his life, to avoid suffering, to distance himself from sinners. Every time what was at stake was whether he would remain faithful to his mission, to seek and to save the lost, to risk his life for this, or if he would spare himself and go his own way. Because he chose God's will every time, he was "without sin," as it says here. Jesus' sinlessness was thus not an attribute or quality which he had "by nature", so to speak, as the Son of God –

perhaps by virtue of his pure birth, but rather consisted in repeatedly new decisions, in a repeatedly obedient Yes to God's difficult path. "He learned obedience through what he suffered" (Heb. 5:8), the writer says of him.

We see him in the Garden of Gethsemane where, facing the greatest hostility that conspired against him, once more he dealt with the tempting question whether there might be another way out for him and therefore also for his disciples, whether he would be spared this unspeakably bitter end. "I am deeply grieved, even to death" (Mt. 26:38), he says to his disciples, and then he prays, "My Father, if it is possible, let this cup pass from me; yet not what I want but what you want" (Mt. 26:39). Nowhere do I find him so close to me than in this perplexity, if it absolutely had to be this way, and at the same time I see how different he is in this temptation than I would be – in his obedient acceptance of God's will.

II.

**In Jesus Christ we have the one we need. He is tempted as we are. He knows our weaknesses.**

In body and soul he underwent what it means to be perplexed and tempted, and therefore he knows how difficult it is to withstand temptation and not to stumble or be ruined. For that reason he does stand speechless before us whenever we do not resist temptation, but succumb to it. In Jesus Christ we are not dealing with one "who is unable to sympathize with our weaknesses," as it says here. Not only does he have sympathy, not only does he feel for us when we experience temptations and are not equal to them, when we cannot cope with the struggle anymore, when we want to give up, but he is truly with us. He knows how difficult the situation is, and he also knows how painful it can be when we have not dealt with it. He bears the burden with us and he suffers with us.

"Because he himself was tested by what he suffered, he is able to help those who are being tested" (Heb. 2:18), it says of him. He does not reproach us for our failure – how could you? – but also does not excuse it – it happened once. Instead, he, God's Son, stays with us as we undergo testing, so that we do not have to give in to it. It is not a powerless sympathy, but an active one.

What are our tests, or temptations? The writer of the Letter to the Hebrews was thinking especially of the temptation to leave Christ and his church. And we know something of that ourselves. We are constantly dealing with this mistrust that is difficult to take because it is vague and never expressed. It is a mistrust that we are not completely reliable because our true commitment is to the church. Somehow that consistently goes with the territory. Perhaps that is due to persons taking certain actions to which we are not privy, ecclesiastically-related. One could stand that, but obviously it carries over to the next generation. Then the temptation is there: Should one not perhaps, as a church, postpone the issue? One should not leave the church immediately, but one should not also, in the end, attend worship and leave it to the children to make the decision later.

The Lord knows how weak our faith is, how little we oppose here. He suffers with and from this weakness of our faith. He says to us, I understand: the temptation to be like others and to take the easier path, to avoid conflicts, and to be spared the cross. But believe me, the exchange is not worth it.

Or we are disappointed in the church and our own congregation. There are so few truly authentic lives, so much triviality and meaningless disputes. And we are prone to disparaging criticism and hear praise for other congregations which enjoy much more light and attention. Again, Jesus comes to us having experienced all the disappointments with his disciples who, over and over again, displayed a new testing for him, whether or not he should abandon them and seek a more convincing circle of followers. "You faithless and perverse generation, how much longer must I be with you? How much longer must I put up with you?" (Mt. 17:17), we hear Jesus say to his disciples. His disappointment was greater than ours can be, and he did not succumb to it. He stood by his disciples, he stood by these not so special people. He is not ashamed to call them his brothers. And now perhaps we also can stand by them.

Or, the confusion of the world becomes a test for us: the mad arms race, the primitive stone age mentality, the criminal misuse of power, the ruthless plunder of nature, the untruthful propaganda, the incitement of hearts, the irreverence for the unborn, the shattering of norms. Will the devil have the last word in this world? The temptation is there: Don't get so excited. You can't change anything. There's no point to it anyway. And again Jesus is there, tempted as we are: a discrete bow before the devil (entirely in confidence) and with that the quiet acknowledgement that he, not God, is the true ruler of the world, and that the world can certainly be changed, but with all the changes the old world will remain. Jesus did not bow before the devil, and he suffers for our being prone to resignation and hopelessness, and simply does not abandon us.

Or when the ingratitude of persons to you – perhaps your own children – is a temptation to become bitter. Again, there is Jesus who had made ten men healthy, and only one of them returned to thank him, so that, disappointed, he asked, "But the other nine, where are they? Was none of them found to return and give praise to God except this foreigner?" (Lk. 17:17b-18). He knows how painful such ingratitude can be and how susceptible we are to bitter thoughts. It is good that he does not leave us alone with our weakness and susceptibility.

III.

**In Jesus Christ we have the one we need. He is tempted as we are. He knows our weaknesses. We can come to him anytime.**

We do not need to hide from such a Lord. He has gone through the same things we have, and he did not face them effortlessly, but rather he struggled and wept. He sweated blood, cried out to God, and was grieved to death. We can put our confidence in such a Lord. We cannot show him anything new. With him we can be who we truly are: weak in faith, feeble, and falling down over and over again. Finally, he is one before whom we do not need to pretend, before whom we do not have to be strong, but may be weak. We are called upon to do so: "Let us therefore approach the throne of grace with boldness, so that we may receive mercy and find grace to help in time of need."

Those words are addressed to us, the church. We step up to the throne of grace, that is, to him, every time we worship. We may approach him with confidence and openness. We have the right to tell him everything, in fact, as things truly are, what our situation really is, what is unfinished, our repeated failures. We may share with him our fears and our bitterness, our thoughts of hopelessness, concern for our children, our loneliness. We need not be ashamed before him – with empty hands and worn out hearts. We have nothing to bring, but everything to receive: mercy when we receive his body and blood, and hear the words: Given for you, poured out for you for the forgiveness of sins. And we receive grace, the strength to continue, help in the hour of temptation when God seems absent. Because we need him so much, then "let us hold fast to our confession" in worship where we, as simple as it may be, encounter him who never abandons us, in life and in death, in our times of testing and in the final temptation. There is no one like him. Amen.

# Afterword

His sermons were a special event. Whoever attended a service in which Werner Krusche preached went home comforted and encouraged. In the words of this preacher the Gospel came to shine. Whoever preaches should give people the invitation of Jesus Christ, he said, following the words of Jesus, "Come to me, all who labor and are heavy laden, and I will give you rest" (Mt. 11:28). The sermon which witnesses to the invitation of Christ wants to show people that Christ is their brother and they are his brothers and sisters. Everyone is invited – the people who come to the service of God on Sunday morning and the people to whom Jesus Christ has become a stranger. They, especially they, were always in Krusche's mind during his sermons.

Werner Krusche was my bishop. At that time I lived in Halle on the Saale in eastern Germany and belonged to the Protestant Church of the Church Province of Saxony where Krusche was bishop from 1968 to 1983. I experienced him from the perspective of the theology student, then as a vicar, and then as an assistant at the Theological Faculty of the Martin Luther University in Halle-Wittenberg. I have been fortunate to hear both his sermons and his lectures. Wherever Krusche spoke or preached, we went. We had the feeling that something important was being said here, something that shouldn't be missed, if at all possible.

People like him were not often found in the gray everyday life of the GDR. You could trust his words. You could feel the criticism of the political situation that surrounded us. He know how to make ideological errors perceptible, unobtrusive, and often with a fine sense of humor. The spiritual horizon, in which all things in life can be recognized in their relationship to God, was important to him. In his sermons and also in his lectures he would always come back to the question of what God intends to do with us – what he gives us, what needs us for, what he expects from us, how he sets us free. The ugly situation behind the wall and barbed wire that we found ourselves in was reflected in the biblical texts about which he preached. As a result, our situation lost its claim to absoluteness and the associated pressure. We got fresh courage to hold on to faith and to Christian witness in the world of atheism.

At the end of a vicariate – the period of formation in a parish – the graduates went through a period of preparation for their ordination by the bishop. In November 1974 I took part in this course at a conference center of our church in the middle of the woods of an impressive mountain landscape. Werner Krusche took a week just to talk to us; he was only there for us these days. We talked about the tasks that awaited us in the pastoral office. We read the Bible and the confessions of the Church's faith together. We celebrated worship together.

Of course, it was also about preaching. It was particularly important to him that people thought about it. Whoever preaches, he told us, needs to know that the biblical text is addressed first to him or her who will preach. The pastor is the first addressee of such a text. He or she can only comfort or admonish others if he or she allows himself or herself to be comforted and admonished by the Bible. That is why the pastor should never only read the Bible professionally; rather, he or she needs regular Bible reading without having to think about the benefits for the work in the congregation.

I still remember a second piece of advice from the bishop, and it has been with me all my life: we should start preparing for a sermon on Monday before the following Sunday, at the latest. We have to read and settle into the text for the sermon. The text should accompany us in all our projects and endeavors, and run like a red thread throughout the week. The dialogue between the text and our situation would almost automatically arise in this way. We would always discover new things and would not have to be afraid of giving a spiritually blind, boring sermon.

The sermons of Werner Krusche can be seen as having been created according to this rule. They are not spiritually blind or boring. Although they were preached many years ago, they have remained alive, thanks to the inherent luminosity of the gospel. When he published his first volume of sermons in 1982, Krusche asked himself whether it would be wise to print the sermons he had given, for sermons are meant to be heard and not to be read. They are by their very nature an "oral word". But contrary to what the bishop might have guessed at the time, his printed sermons have retained astonishingly much of the character of the oral word. They have spoken to many people because they have become a living word to them again. May the American readers also experience this!

Michael Beintker
Münster/Westphalia
Spring 2021

www.ingramcontent.com/pod-product-compliance
Lightning Source LLC
Chambersburg PA
CBHW071445070526
44578CB00001B/218